the fourth of july

LABOR DAY

halloween

THANKSGIVING

hanukkah

christmas

# BON APPÉTIT

## HOLIDAYS

# BON APPÉTIT

# HOLIDAYS

*from the editors of Bon Appétit*

Condé Nast Books · Pantheon
New York

# CONTENTS

ISBN 0-679-44278-2

Printed in the United States of America

FIRST EDITION
2 4 6 8 9 7 5 3 1

# INTRODUCTION

HOLIDAYS ARE THE BEST DAYS. DOWN THE STRETCH OF ORDINARY TIMES THEY SHINE BRIGHTLY—FIREWORKS, HANUKKAH MENORAHS, CHRISTMAS TREES AND SPARKLING CHAMPAGNE LIGHTING OUR WAY THROUGH THE YEAR. MONTH TO MONTH, HOLIDAYS ARE OCCASIONS THAT JOIN OLD FRIENDS, NEW FRIENDS AND FAMILY, BRINGING US TOGETHER TO SHARE TRADITIONS, GOOD TIMES AND, OF COURSE, FOOD. AS HOLIDAYS ANCHOR OUR LIVES SO DOES WHAT WE COOK AND EAT FOR THOSE CELEBRATIONS CONNECT US TO THEM OVER THE YEARS AND THE GENERATIONS. THAT'S WHY WE'VE COMPILED THIS COLLECTION OF SPECIAL RECIPES, EACH DESIGNED TO BRING A SPECIAL DAY, BE IT EASTER, PASSOVER, THANKSGIVING OR NEW YEAR'S EVE INTO CLEAR AND MEMORABLE FOCUS.

HERE, COLLECTED IN ONE VOLUME, IS TWELVE MONTHS' WORTH OF GOOD TIMES, BEGINNING WITH THE FIRST DAY OF THE NEW YEAR AND ENDING WITH THE FINAL STROKE OF MIDNIGHT, A YEAR AND SIXTEEN FABULOUS HOLIDAYS LATER.

EACH HOLIDAY IS CENTERED AROUND A CAREFULLY CONSIDERED MENU, ONE THAT SPEAKS TO THE TRADITIONS OF THE DAY WHILE KEEPING UP WITH THE NEW AND KEEPING PACE WITH HECTIC SCHEDULES. SOME OF THE HOLIDAYS INCLUDE A SECOND MENU OFFERING A DIFFERENT APPROACH TO THE CELEBRATION; OTHERS FEATURE A STEP-BY-STEP "COOKING CLASS" TO A DISH THAT SEEMS ESPECIALLY FITTING (LIKE MOLDED CHOCOLATE EGGS WITH CARAMEL CENTERS FOR EASTER AND THE BEST FRIED CHICKEN WE'VE EVER TASTED FOR THE FOURTH OF JULY). STILL OTHERS OFFER ADDITIONAL RECIPES THAT SERVE TO ROUND OUT THE HOLIDAY FARE, INCLUDING A COLLECTION OF SPECIAL DESSERTS FOR PASSOVER, TWO ADDITIONAL TURKEY RECIPES FOR THANKSGIVING AND A NUMBER OF IDEAS FOR CHRISTMAS GIFTS THAT YOU MAKE IN YOUR KITCHEN. IN ADDITION, YOU'LL FIND ADVICE, TIPS AND STRATEGIES THROUGHOUT, FROM WHAT TO INCLUDE WHEN STOCKING THE BAR FOR A BIG PARTY TO CLEVER IDEAS FOR HALLOWEEN DECORATING.

CELEBRATING HOLIDAYS IS ABOUT CARRYING ON TRADITIONS AND STARTING YOUR OWN. IT'S ABOUT GETTING TOGETHER WITH ALL THE FRIENDS AND FAMILY THERE WOULD NEVER BE ENOUGH TIME FOR OTHERWISE. AND IT'S ABOUT COOKING, AND MAKING FOODS THAT LINK THE PAST WITH THE PRESENT. IT'S WHAT THIS BOOK IS ABOUT, JUST AS IT IS ABOUT THE GOOD TIMES, THE MEMORIES AND THE TRADITIONAL, TREASURED AND WONDERFUL DISHES AND FOOD AROUND WHICH ALL THE HOLIDAYS REVOLVE.

**1**
JAN

# NEW YEAR'S DAY

IF YOU MAKE ONLY ONE RESOLUTION THIS YEAR, MAKE IT ONE YOU'RE GOING TO LIKE KEEPING. HOW ABOUT RESOLVING TO GATHER YOUR NEAREST AND DEAREST AROUND YOU MORE OFTEN AND COOK THEM WONDERFUL FOOD, DOING SO WITH A CASUAL GRACE THAT LEAVES EVERYONE— YOURSELF INCLUDED—RELAXED, HAPPY AND WELL FED? COMPARED WITH LAST YEAR'S VOW TO READ THE WORLD'S 100 GREATEST BOOKS IN THEIR ORIGINAL LANGUAGES, THIS ONE YOU MAY WELL MANAGE, NOT TO MENTION ENJOY.

BEGIN YOUR YEAR OF NEW AND IMPROVED ENTERTAINING AS SOON AS THE CALENDAR ALLOWS WITH A STYLISH *AND* STRESS-FREE NEW YEAR'S DAY SUPPER. PRUDENTLY DESIGNED AS A HELP-YOURSELF BUFFET TO ACCOMMODATE DROP-IN GUESTS AND BALL GAMES, THIS SIMPLE-TO-COOK FEAST COMBINES LIGHTER NIBBLES (FOR THOSE RESOLVED TO LOSE A POUND—OR TEN) ALONG WITH HEARTIER FARE (FOR THOSE BEGINNING THEIR DIETS TOMORROW), AND DISHES CHOSEN FOR THEIR TRADITIONAL ASSOCIATIONS WITH THE NEW YEAR AND THE GOOD LUCK WE ALL HOPE IT BRINGS. WHEN THE YEAR GETS ITS START WITH A PARTY THIS EASY AND FOOD THIS DELICIOUS, YOU KNOW IT'S GOING TO BE A GOOD ONE.

OPPOSITE: CRANBERRY-PECAN POUND CAKE (LEFT) AND VICTORIA TART WITH RUM WHIPPED CREAM (RIGHT).

## Sesame Cheese Spread with Crudités

*Make this savory spread (below) up to a day ahead.*

makes about 1 cup

1   8-OUNCE PACKAGE CREAM CHEESE, ROOM TEMPERATURE
1   GREEN ONION, MINCED
1   TABLESPOON SOY SAUCE
1   TABLESPOON MINCED PEELED FRESH GINGER
1   TABLESPOON DRY SHERRY
¼   CUP SESAME SEEDS, TOASTED
    ASSORTED CRUDITÉS (BROCCOLI, CAULIFLOWER, CARROTS, RADISHES, BELL PEPPERS)

Throughly combine first 5 ingredients in medium bowl. Chill until beginning to firm, about 30 minutes. Using spatula as aid, shape mixture into ball in bowl. Place sesame seeds in shallow dish. Place cheese ball on seeds and roll around to coat completely. *(Can be prepared 1 day ahead. Cover and refrigerate. Bring to room temperature before serving.)* Serve with crudités.

## Spicy-Smoky Peanuts

*These roasted peanuts have a rich, smoky flavor that makes them a good accompaniment to cocktails.*

makes 2 cups

2   CUPS HUSKED SHELLED RAW SPANISH PEANUTS (ABOUT 10 OUNCES)
4   TEASPOONS WORCESTERSHIRE SAUCE
1   TABLESPOON LIQUID SMOKE FLAVORING*

2   TABLESPOONS (¼ STICK) BUTTER
2   TEASPOONS DISTILLED WHITE VINEGAR
2   TEASPOONS HOT PEPPER SAUCE (SUCH AS TABASCO)
¾   TEASPOON SALT
⅛   TEASPOON CAYENNE PEPPER

Line jelly roll pan with foil. Toss peanuts, Worcestershire sauce and liquid smoke in pan. Let marinate at room temperature, stirring occasionally, about 30 minutes.

Position rack in center of oven and preheat to 325°F. Melt butter in heavy large skillet over medium-low heat. Cool slightly. Stir in vinegar, hot pepper sauce, salt and cayenne. Return skillet to heat. Scrape in nuts and marinade. Stir to coat nuts, about 30 seconds. Return nut mixture to jelly roll pan. Bake until golden brown, stirring occasionally, about 20 minutes. Transfer pan to rack and cool. Let stand uncovered 6 hours to dry. *(Can be made 1 week ahead. Store nuts in airtight container at room temperature.)*

*A smoke-flavored liquid seasoning available at many supermarkets.

## Natchez Jambalaya

*This zesty, colorful mélange of chicken, shrimp, sausage and rice can be assembled early in the day (or even the day before the party) and finished in the oven when ready to serve. Champagne makes a refreshing and suitably festive drink.*

**12 servings**

6 TABLESPOONS VEGETABLE OIL

1 POUND SMOKED OR CAJUN SAUSAGE (SUCH AS ANDOUILLE), CUT INTO ½-INCH-THICK SLICES

3½ POUNDS BONELESS CHICKEN BREASTS OR THIGHS, CUT INTO 2- TO 3-INCH PIECES

1 TEASPOON CAYENNE PEPPER

3 LARGE CELERY STALKS, THINLY SLICED

2 LARGE ONIONS, COARSELY CHOPPED

2 LARGE GREEN BELL PEPPERS, CUT INTO ¾-INCH PIECES

6 GARLIC CLOVES, MINCED

1 TABLESPOON DRIED THYME

3 CUPS LONG-GRAIN RICE

3 16-OUNCE CANS ITALIAN PLUM TOMATOES

2 TO 3½ CUPS CANNED CHICKEN BROTH

2 CUPS BOTTLED CLAM JUICE

1 POUND MEDIUM SHRIMP, PEELED AND DEVEINED

HOT PEPPER SAUCE, SUCH AS TABASCO

1 BUNCH GREEN ONIONS, THINLY SLICED

Heat 3 tablespoons oil in heavy large skillet over medium heat. Add sausage and sauté until brown, about 8 minutes. Transfer sausage to bowl using slotted spoon; reserve sausage drippings. Sprinkle both sides of chicken pieces with cayenne pepper. Add to skillet with sausage drippings and sauté until brown and cooked through, turning occasionally, about 5 minutes. Transfer chicken to bowl with sausage.

Heat remaining 3 tablespoons oil in same skillet over medium heat. Add celery, onions and bell peppers and cook until onions are transparent, stirring occasionally, about 8 minutes. Add garlic and cook 1 minute. Stir in thyme. Add rice to skillet and stir until coated with oil. Divide rice mixture between two 9 x 13-inch baking dishes. Cover with foil. *(Can be prepared 1 day ahead. Refrigerate rice, chicken and sausage separately. Bring to room temperature before continuing.)*

Preheat oven to 350°F. Drain juices from 1 tomato can; place tomatoes in heavy large saucepan. Add remaining tomatoes with their juices, 2 cups chicken broth and clam juice. Bring to boil, breaking up tomatoes with spoon. Divide between baking dishes. Cover with foil. Bake 35 minutes.

Remove from oven and arrange shrimp, sausage and chicken over rice. If rice has absorbed most of liquid, add ¾ cup more chicken broth to each baking dish. Cover and bake until rice is tender, shrimp are cooked through and chicken is hot, about 15 minutes.

Season jambalaya with hot pepper sauce and salt. Transfer to serving platter. Sprinkle with green onions.

## Double Corn Mini Muffins

*These moist, golden corn muffins can also be baked in 12 to 14 standard-size muffin cups for about 15 minutes. They freeze well and are easily and quickly reheated in a low oven or in a microwave.*

**makes 28**

1 CUP ALL PURPOSE FLOUR

1 CUP YELLOW CORNMEAL

2 TABLESPOONS GOLDEN BROWN SUGAR

1 TABLESPOON BAKING POWDER

½ TEASPOON BAKING SODA

½ TEASPOON SALT

1 8½-OUNCE CAN CREAMED CORN

½ CUP BUTTERMILK

1 EGG

¼ CUP (½ STICK) BUTTER, MELTED

Position rack in center of oven and preheat to 425°F. Butter 28 mini muffin cups. Mix first 6 ingredients in large bowl. Whisk creamed corn, buttermilk and egg in another bowl until well combined. Whisk in ¼ cup melted butter. Form well in center of dry ingredients. Add buttermilk mixture to well and stir just until all ingredients are moist. Spoon batter into prepared muffin cups, filling ¾ full. Bake until golden brown, about 10 minutes. Remove muffins from cups and cool slightly on rack. *(Can be prepared 2 weeks ahead. Cool completely. Wrap tightly and freeze. Thaw, then wrap in foil and rewarm in 300°F oven or cover with plastic and rewarm in microwave.)* Serve warm.

## Black-eyed Pea Salad

*Tradition has it that black-eyed peas bring good luck when eaten on New Year's Day. If you are unable to find young dandelion greens, substitute mustard greens or use more arugula.*

**12 servings**

VINAIGRETTE

⅓  CUP RED WINE VINEGAR

1½  TABLESPOONS COARSE-GRAINED DIJON MUSTARD

2½  TEASPOONS SUGAR

1  CUP OLIVE OIL

1½  GARLIC CLOVES, MINCED

1¾  TEASPOONS SALT

¾  TEASPOON PEPPER

SALAD

12  OUNCES DRIED BLACK-EYED PEAS OR THREE 10-OUNCE PACKAGES FROZEN, COOKED ACCORDING TO PACKAGE INSTRUCTIONS, DRAINED

2  MEDIUM-SIZE RED BELL PEPPERS, DICED

⅓  CUP CHOPPED FRESH ITALIAN PARSLEY

4  BUNCHES ARUGULA

2  BUNCHES YOUNG DANDELION GREENS, STEMMED MUSTARD GREENS OR ARUGULA

1  CUP THINLY SLICED RED ONION

FOR VINAIGRETTE: Whisk vinegar, mustard and sugar in medium bowl until sugar dissolves. Gradually whisk in oil. Add garlic, salt and pepper. *(Can be prepared 2 days ahead. Cover and chill. Bring to room temperature before using.)*

FOR SALAD: Combine black-eyed peas, bell peppers and all but 1 tablespoon Italian parsley in large bowl. Add 1 cup vinaigrette and toss. Refrigerate at least 2 and up to 6 hours.

Toss arugula and dandelion greens with remaining vinaigrette. Arrange on large rimmed platter. Spoon black-eyed pea salad into center of platter. Sprinkle with remaining parsley. Garnish with red onion and serve.

## Cranberry-Pecan Pound Cake

*This rich pound cake studded with cranberries and toasted pecans cuts into lovely, neat slices, making it perfect for a buffet. It's best if the flavors are allowed to mellow for a day or two before serving.*

**20 servings**

1  CUP CHOPPED PECANS (ABOUT 5 OUNCES)

1½  CUPS CRANBERRIES

2  CUPS SUGAR

1  CUP (2 STICKS) UNSALTED BUTTER, ROOM TEMPERATURE

5  LARGE EGGS

¼  CUP SOUR CREAM

¼  CUP ORANGE LIQUEUR, SUCH AS GRAND MARNIER OR TRIPLE SEC

2  TEASPOONS VANILLA EXTRACT

1  TEASPOON GRATED ORANGE PEEL

1¼  CUPS ALL PURPOSE FLOUR

1  CUP CAKE FLOUR

½  TEASPOON SALT

POWDERED SUGAR

Postition rack in center of oven and preheat to 350°F. Butter and flour 2½-quart tube cake pan or two 8½ x 4½-inch loaf pans. Place pecans on cookie sheet and bake until lightly colored and fragrant, about 10 minutes. Cool. Coarsely chop cranberries.

Using electric mixer, beat sugar and butter in large bowl until light and fluffy, scraping sides of bowl once. Beat in eggs 1 at a time. Beat in sour cream, then liqueur, vanilla and orange peel. Sift all purpose flour, cake flour and salt together. With mixer on low speed, add dry ingredients to egg mixture and stop when all flour has been added. Mix by hand until just combined. Fold in pecans and cranberries. Pour batter into prepared cake pan. Tap pan on counter to release any air bubbles. Bake until tester inserted in center comes out clean, about 45 minutes for loaf pans and about 1 hour for tube pan.

Cool cake in pan 10 minutes. Turn out onto rack and cool completely. Wrap in plastic and refrigerate at least 1 and up to 3 days. *(Can be frozen up to 1 month.)* Dust cake lightly with powdered sugar before serving.

OPPOSITE: NATCHEZ JAMBALAYA; BLACK-EYED PEA SALAD; AND DOUBLE CORN MINI MUFFINS.

## Victoria Tart

*Cut this delectable chocolate tart into slim wedges, and set the rum-flavored whipped cream out in a nice bowl so guests can spoon some alongside each serving.*

**12 servings**

CRUST

1¼ CUPS ALL PURPOSE FLOUR
1 TABLESPOON SUGAR
¼ TEASPOON SALT
½ CUP (1 STICK) UNSALTED BUTTER, CHILLED, CUT INTO SMALL PIECES
1 EGG YOLK
1 TABLESPOON (OR MORE) COLD WATER

FILLING

2 OUNCES UNSWEETENED CHOCOLATE
½ CUP (1 STICK) UNSALTED BUTTER
1 TEASPOON INSTANT ESPRESSO POWDER
2 EGGS
¾ CUP SUGAR
¼ CUP PACKED GOLDEN BROWN SUGAR
¼ CUP ALL PURPOSE FLOUR
2 TEASPOONS VANILLA EXTRACT
PINCH OF SALT
RUM WHIPPED CREAM (SEE RECIPE AT RIGHT)

FOR CRUST: Mix flour, sugar and salt in processor. Distribute butter evenly over flour mixture. Process until mixture resembles coarse meal, using 12 on/off turns. Beat egg yolk and 1 tablespoon water in small bowl. With machine running, pour egg mixture through feed tube and process 5 seconds. If dough is dry and crumbly, add more water 1 teaspoon at a time and blend just until dough begins to come together. Gather dough into ball; flatten into disk. Wrap in plastic and refrigerate at least 30 minutes. *(Can be prepared 2 days ahead.)*

Roll dough out on lightly floured surface to 12-inch-diameter round. Transfer to 9- or 10-inch tart pan with removable bottom. Press dough into sides of pan. Trim edges. Pierce dough with fork. Refrigerate 30 minutes.

Position rack in lowest third of oven and preheat to 425°F. Bake crust until golden brown, about 12 minutes. Cool on rack. *(Can be prepared 1 day ahead. Cover and store at room temperature.)*

FOR FILLING: Position rack in center of oven and preheat to 350°F. Melt chocolate and butter with espresso powder in top of double boiler over simmering water. Remove from over water. Whisk eggs, both sugars, flour, vanilla and salt in large bowl until well blended. Whisk in chocolate mixture. Pour filling into crust. Bake until edges are set and center is soft but not liquid, about 25 minutes. Cool on rack. *(Can be prepared 8 hours ahead. Cover and store at room temperature.)* Serve tart with whipped cream.

## Rum Whipped Cream

**makes about 2 cups**

1 CUP CHILLED WHIPPING CREAM
1 TABLESPOON POWDERED SUGAR
1 TABLESPOON DARK RUM

In chilled bowl, beat cream to soft peaks. Add powdered sugar and rum and beat until blended. *(Can be prepared 3 hours ahead. Refrigerate.)*

## Pear Slices With Blue Cheese

*Using both red and green pears makes the presentation even prettier.*

**12 servings**

3 RIPE BUT FIRM RED BARTLETT PEARS
3 RIPE BUT FIRM BARTLETT OR OTHER GREEN PEARS
½ LEMON
8 OUNCES SPREADABLE BLUE CHEESE, SUCH AS BAVARIAN, MAYTAG OR SAGA, ROOM TEMPERATURE

Core pears; do not peel. Cut into ½-inch-thick slices. Squeeze lemon over cut sides. Spread one side of each pear with blue cheese. Arrange on platter. *(Can be prepared 1 hour ahead. Cover with plastic and refrigerate.)*

# STOCKING *the* BAR

**A** well-stocked bar is ready for any request, whether it's for a Martini or mineral water. For a party like this one, you may want a full bar, with a variety of spirits and mixers, wines, beers and waters. Check your private inventory, make a list of what's required, then supplement as necessary.

Set up the bar where there is plenty of surface area on which to place bottles and glasses. Make sure there is space behind the bar, too, so that the bartender (host, hired or volunteer) can comfortably mix and pour.

In addition to what your guests will be drinking, consider what they'll be drinking from. Four types of glasses should cover the range of drinks: flutes for Champagne, goblets for wine, highballs for tall mixed drinks and double old-fashioneds for whiskey and bourbon.

And don't forget the necessary accessories, including an ice bucket (or two), corkscrews, a Champagne key, swizzle sticks, a shaker, a jigger and an assortment of cocktail garnishes, plus napkins and coasters.

As a rule, the well-stocked bar should have at least the following:

| | |
|---|---|
| Gin | Vodka |
| Scotch Whisky | Whiskey |
| Bourbon | Rum |
| Tequila | Liqueurs |
| Vermouth (dry and sweet) | Wine (red and white) |
| Cognac or other brandy | Beer |

# VALENTINE'S DAY

Love is in the air. Or is it merely the smell of good chocolate? Come the fourteenth of February, the two go hand in hand, as inseparable as Cupid and his bow. Celebrate this happy pairing with something sweet and chocolaty, maybe a batch of homemade fudge or a simply stunning dessert, like the mousse-filled chocolate hearts here. If your loved ones are little ones, consider letting them join you in the kitchen to whip up—and then sample—some heart-shaped lollipops.

If it *is* love in the air, a romantic dinner for two might be just the kind of celebration you had in mind. Clear your schedule, clear the decks and create a quiet candlelit island of love for you and the object of your desire. And since slaving over a hot stove while the significant other slips into a doze at the table is counterproductive, here's a supper that's speedy, light and Champagne-compatible. Once it's on the table, the rest of the magic is up to you and the February moon.

Opposite: Two-Pepper Shrimp; Rice Salad with Dill and Baby Vegetables; and Blackberry Parfaits.

## VALENTINE'S DAY SUPPER *for* TWO

SMOKED SALMON *on*
SOURDOUGH ROUNDS *with*
CAPER-DILL RELISH

CHAMPAGNE

TWO-PEPPER SHRIMP

RICE SALAD *with* DILL *and*
BABY VEGETABLES

GEWÜRZTRAMINER

BLACKBERRY PARFAITS

## Smoked Salmon on Sourdough Rounds with Caper-Dill Relish

*Pretty and tasty, this easy starter (below) takes minutes to make.*

**makes 6**

| | |
|---|---|
| 1½ | TABLESPOONS FINELY CHOPPED WHITE ONION |
| 2 | TEASPOONS DRAINED CAPERS |
| 1½ | TEASPOONS (PACKED) CHOPPED FRESH DILL |
| 1 | TEASPOON DIJON MUSTARD |
| ¾ | TEASPOON FRESH LEMON JUICE |
| 1½ | OUNCES CREAM CHEESE, ROOM TEMPERATURE |
| 6 | THIN SLICES SOURDOUGH BAGUETTE |
| 1½ | OUNCES THINLY SLICED SMOKED SALMON, CUT INTO 6 PIECES |

Stir first 5 ingredients in small bowl to blend. Season with salt and pepper.

Spread cream cheese over baguette slices. Top each with 1 salmon piece, then with generous 1 teaspoon relish. Arrange appetizers on platter.

## Two-Pepper Shrimp

*Crushed red pepper and cracked black pepper give this delicious dish its heat and make the cool rice salad with dill a perfect accompaniment. Offer a fruity Gewürztraminer to drink.*

**2 servings**

| | |
|---|---|
| ½ | POUND UNCOOKED LARGE SHRIMP, PEELED, DEVEINED |
| 2 | TABLESPOONS DRY WHITE WINE |
| 1 | TEASPOON GRATED PEELED FRESH GINGER |
| ¼ | TEASPOON CRACKED BLACK PEPPER |
| | PINCH OF DRIED CRUSHED RED PEPPER |
| 4 | TABLESPOONS RICE VINEGAR |
| 1 | CUP PLUS 1 TABLESPOON COLD WATER |
| 2½ | CUPS SHREDDED ROMAINE LETTUCE |
| 4 | RADISHES, TRIMMED, THINLY SLICED |

¼ CUP BOTTLED CLAM JUICE

1 TEASPOON CORNSTARCH

¼ TEASPOON SALT

PINCH OF SUGAR

2 TEASPOONS OLIVE OIL

½ POUND ONIONS, THINLY SLICED

¼ CUP DRAINED CANNED DICED TOMATOES

1 SMALL GARLIC CLOVE, MINCED

1 TABLESPOON CHOPPED FRESH PARSLEY

Mix shrimp, 1 tablespoon wine, ginger, black pepper and crushed red pepper in medium bowl. Cover and chill 30 minutes. Drain, reserving marinade.

Pour 3½ tablespoons rice vinegar into another medium bowl. Add 1 cup cold water to bowl. Add shredded lettuce and radishes. Let stand 5 minutes. Drain lettuce and radishes.

Whisk clam juice, remaining 1 tablespoon wine and remaining ½ tablespoon vinegar in small bowl to blend. Add cornstarch, salt and sugar; whisk until cornstarch dissolves. Whisk in reserved shrimp marinade. Set aside.

Heat 1 teaspoon olive oil in medium nonstick skillet over medium-high heat. Add shrimp and sauté until just cooked through, about 2 minutes. Using slotted spoon, transfer shrimp to plate. Heat remaining 1 teaspoon oil in same skillet over medium-high heat. Add onions and sauté until beginning to soften, about 4 minutes. Add remaining 1 tablespoon water and stir 1 minute. Add tomatoes and garlic and stir 30 seconds. Rewhisk clam juice mixture to blend. Add to skillet and boil until sauce thickens, about 1 minute. Add shrimp and parsley and toss to coat. Season to taste with salt and pepper. Remove from heat.

Divide lettuce and radishes between 2 plates. Spoon shrimp mixture and sauce over and serve.

## Rice Salad with Dill and Baby Vegetables

**2 servings**

2 OUNCES BABY CARROTS (ABOUT 8), TRIMMED, HALVED LENGTHWISE

4 OUNCES BABY ZUCCHINI OR BABY PATTYPAN SQUASH, ENDS TRIMMED, HALVED

6 TABLESPOONS LONG-GRAIN WHITE RICE

¼ CUP PLAIN LOW-FAT YOGURT

1½ TABLESPOONS CHOPPED FRESH DILL

2 TEASPOONS RICE VINEGAR

½ TEASPOON OLIVE OIL

FRESH DILL SPRIGS (OPTIONAL)

Blanch carrots in medium pot of boiling salted water 1 minute. Add zucchini and cook 1 minute. Using slotted spoon, transfer vegetables to colander. Rinse under cold water; drain well. Add rice to same pot of boiling water. Cook until tender, about 15 minutes. Drain. Rinse under cold water; drain well. Cool to room temperature.

Mix rice, carrots and zucchini in medium bowl. Add yogurt, chopped dill, vinegar and oil. Toss to coat. Season to taste with salt and pepper. *(Can be prepared 6 hours ahead. Cover and refrigerate.)* Garnish with dill sprigs, if desired.

## Blackberry Parfaits

*An almond-scented pudding layered with blackberries and blackberry preserves makes a nice finale. (The recipe makes two extra parfaits, which you may want to enjoy on February 15.)*

**4 servings**

¼ CUP ALL-FRUIT BLACKBERRY SPREAD

2 TABLESPOONS AMARETTO LIQUEUR

1½ TEASPOONS VANILLA EXTRACT

⅓ CUP SUGAR

2 TABLESPOONS ALL PURPOSE FLOUR

2 TABLESPOONS CORNSTARCH

PINCH OF SALT

2¼ CUPS LOW-FAT (1%) MILK

1 LARGE EGG

1 TEASPOON UNSALTED BUTTER

¼ TEASPOON ALMOND EXTRACT

2 CUPS (ABOUT) FROZEN BLACKBERRIES, THAWED

Whisk blackberry spread, 1 tablespoon amaretto and 1 teaspoon vanilla in small bowl until smooth.

Whisk sugar, flour, cornstarch and salt in heavy medium saucepan to blend. Gradually whisk in milk. Whisk in egg. Add butter. Whisk over medium heat until mixture comes to boil and thickens, about 6 minutes. Boil 1 minute longer, whisking constantly. Remove from heat. Whisk in almond extract, 1 remaining tablespoon amaretto and ½ teaspoon vanilla.

Spoon 1 teaspoon blackberry spread mixture into bottom of each of four 1-cup stemmed glasses. Top each with 4 blackberries, then with about 3 tablespoons hot pudding. Repeat layering twice more. Divide any remaining blackberries among glasses. Refrigerate until cold, about 3 hours. *(Blackberry parfaits can be prepared 1 day ahead. Keep refrigerated.)*

# HOW *to* MAKE *a* CLASSIC CANDY

LOVE AND CHOCOLATE ARE A CLASSIC PAIR, A PERFECT MATCH. STILL, EVEN THE BEST RELATIONSHIP CAN USE A SPARK NOW AND THEN. HERE'S JUST THE THING: RICH CHOCOLATE FUDGE (BELOW) ENLIVENED WITH ESPRESSO, WALNUTS AND CINNAMON. IT'S IDEAL FOR VALENTINE'S DAY, WHEN EVERY ROMANCE DESERVES A LITTLE BIT OF SWEETENING.

## *Mocha-Spice Fudge*

**makes about 24 pieces**

2 TABLESPOONS (¼ STICK) UNSALTED BUTTER, ROOM TEMPERATURE

¼ CUP WATER

3 TABLESPOONS INSTANT ESPRESSO POWDER OR INSTANT COFFEE POWDER

1 CUP SUGAR

1 CUP FIRMLY PACKED GOLDEN BROWN SUGAR

¾ CUP WHIPPING CREAM

¼ CUP LIGHT CORN SYRUP

½ TEASPOON CREAM OF TARTAR

 PINCH OF SALT

7 OUNCES BITTERSWEET (NOT UNSWEETENED) OR SEMISWEET CHOCOLATE, VERY FINELY CHOPPED

1 TEASPOON VANILLA EXTRACT

½ TEASPOON GROUND CINNAMON

1 CUP COARSELY CHOPPED WALNUTS

Line 8-inch square glass baking dish with foil, extending over sides. Rub ½ tablespoon butter over foil. Mix ¼ cup water and espresso powder in heavy 3-quart saucepan until powder is dissolved. Add sugar, brown sugar, cream, corn syrup, cream of tartar and salt. Using wooden spoon, stir constantly over medium-low heat until sugar dissolves, about 8 minutes; do not boil. With pastry brush dipped into water, brush down any sugar crystals from sides of pan. Remove mixture from heat. Add chopped chocolate; stir until melted and smooth.

Attach clip-on candy thermometer to side of pan. Place pan over medium-low heat; cook without stirring until thermometer registers 238°F, adjusting heat as necessary so that mixture bubbles gently, about 25 minutes.

Remove pan from heat. Add remaining 1½ tablespoons butter, vanilla extract and cinnamon and stir just until blended. Immediately pour mixture into bowl of heavy-duty mixer; do not scrape pan. Set bowl over larger bowl filled with cool water. Let stand until candy thermometer inserted into center of fudge registers 110°F, about 50 minutes; do not stir.

Attach bowl to mixer fitted with paddle attachment. Beat on low speed until mixture lightens in color and loses some sheen, about 15 minutes. Add chopped nuts and beat until combined. Turn out fudge into prepared dish (fudge will be sticky). Using buttered fingertips, press fudge into dish. Let stand until set, about 2 hours.

Lift fudge from dish. Using 1½-inch cookie cutters, cut into shapes. (*Can be made 10 days ahead. Store in airtight container at room temperature.*)

1 After dissolving the sugar in the candy mixture, dip a pastry brush into water and use it to brush down any sugar crystals that may be clinging to the sides of the pan.

2 To make sure the sugar has dissolved, spoon some slightly cooled mixture onto a plate. Rub between fingers; it should feel smooth, with no sugar granules.

3 Cook the mixture, without stirring, over medium-low heat to a temperature of 238°F, adjusting heat so that the mixture bubbles gently.

4 After cooling the fudge to 110°F, beat the mixture until it lightens in color and loses some sheen, approximately 15 minutes.

5 After fudge sets, lift it from the pan, using the foil lining as an aid. Fold down the foil sides; then use small cookie cutters to cut out desired shapes.

## TIPS *for* SUCCESS

Make sure the sugar in the candy mixture is completely dissolved before boiling the mixture. To test, spoon a small amount onto a plate and cool slightly. Rub mixture between fingertips; it should feel smooth, with no traces of granules. It is also crucial not to stir the mixture while cooking; stirring can cause sugar crystals, making the fudge grainy.

Use an accurate clip-on thermometer graduated in one- or two-degree increments. A candy thermometer with a bottom foot (such as a Taylor) can be left in the pan while the mixture is cooking, since the bulb of the thermometer is suspended in the mixture.

Altitude affects boiling temperature (212°F). To get a precise reading, set your thermometer in a small pot of water and bring to a boil. Adjust the temperatures given in the recipe by the amount the reading deviates from 212°F. For example, if your water boils at 210°F, subtract two degrees from the temperatures in the recipe.

Do not scrape the pan sides when pouring out the fudge. Some sugar crystals may be clinging to the pan. If the crystals are mixed into the fudge, it could become grainy.

Before it is beaten, fudge must be cooled without being stirred. If stirred while too warm, sugar crystals will form, making the fudge grainy.

# MORE SWEETS *for the* SWEET

FLOWERS, CARDS WITH LACY EDGES AND WELL-INTEN- TIONED SAYINGS, CANDLE- LIGHT AND THE POP OF A CHAM- PAGNE CORK—THIS IS THE STUFF OF VALENTINE'S DAY. BUT NONE OF THESE IS MORE EVOCATIVE OF THE HOLIDAY OF LOVE THAN CHOCOLATE.

A BOX OF CHOCOLATES IS NICE; ONE OF THESE SPECTACULAR CHOCOLATE DESSERTS IS EVEN BETTER. EACH IS SHAPED LIKE A HEART AND MAKES A DELICIOUS, MEMORABLE CELEBRATION OF THE DAY.

## White-Chocolate Custard Kissing Cookies

*The extra custard makes a great ice cream-type snack. If a cookie cutter isn't available, cut out a four-inch heart-shaped template from cardboard.*

makes 8

### CUSTARD

2¼ CUPS CHILLED WHIPPING CREAM

1¼ CUPS HALF AND HALF

1 VANILLA BEAN, SPLIT LENGTHWISE

12 LARGE EGG YOLKS

½ CUP SUGAR

2 OUNCES GOOD-QUALITY WHITE CHOCOLATE (SUCH AS LINDT OR BAKER'S), FINELY CHOPPED

### COOKIES

3 CUPS ALL PURPOSE FLOUR

¾ TEASPOON BAKING POWDER

¼ TEASPOON SALT

1¼ CUPS (2½ STICKS) UNSALTED BUTTER, ROOM TEMPERATURE

1 CUP SUGAR

1 LARGE EGG

2 TABLESPOONS WHIPPING CREAM

2½ TEASPOONS VANILLA EXTRACT

### SAUCE

2 12-OUNCE BASKETS STRAWBERRIES, HULLED, SLICED OR 1 POUND FROZEN, UNSWEETENED, THAWED

½ CUP SUGAR

2 TABLESPOONS DARK RUM

1 CINNAMON STICK

FRESH MINT LEAVES

FOR CUSTARD: Butter 15 x 10 x ¾-inch baking sheet. Line sheet with waxed paper. Combine 1¼ cups cream and half and half in heavy large saucepan. Scrape in seeds from vanilla bean; add bean. Bring to boil over high heat. Remove from heat. Cover; let mixture steep for 15 minutes.

Using electric mixer at high speed, beat yolks and sugar in large bowl until thick and fluffy, about 5 minutes. Reduce mixer speed to low; gradually beat hot cream mixture into yolk mixture. Return yolk mixture to same saucepan. Stir over medium heat until custard thickens, about 6 minutes; do not boil. Strain custard into large bowl. Add white chocolate and stir until melted and smooth.

Refrigerate custard until cooled to room temperature, whisking occasion- ally, about 25 minutes. Beat remaining 1 cup whipping cream until medium- firm peaks form. Fold whipped cream into custard mixture in 2 additions. Spread mixture evenly in prepared baking sheet. Freeze until firm, about 6 hours. *(Can be prepared 1 day ahead. Cover and keep frozen.)*

FOR COOKIES: Preheat oven to 350°F. Butter 2 heavy large cookie sheets. Sift flour, baking powder and salt into medium bowl. Using electric mixer, beat butter in large bowl until smooth. Gradually add sugar and beat until light and fluffy. Add egg, cream and vanilla extract and beat until blended. Add dry ingredients and mix just until blended. Divide dough in half; form into disks. Wrap tightly in plastic and refrigerate cookie dough 15 minutes.

Roll out 1 dough piece on lightly floured surface to ¼-inch thickness (about 11-inch round), turning dough and flouring board as necessary to prevent sticking. Using 4-inch heart- shaped cutter, cut out 8 cookies. Transfer cookies to 1 prepared cookie sheet, spacing evenly. Repeat rolling and cutting with remaining dough. Transfer cookies to second sheet.

Bake cookies until golden brown on edges and firm in center, about 8 minutes. Let cool on sheets 5 minutes. Transfer cookies to rack and cool com- pletely. *(Can be prepared 1 day ahead. Store airtight at room temperature.)*

FOR SAUCE: Combine strawberries, sugar, dark rum and cinnamon stick in heavy large skillet. Cook over high heat until sauce thickens and coats spoon, stirring often, about 10 minutes. Transfer sauce to bowl. Cover and refrigerate until cold, at least 2 hours. *(Can be prepared 1 day ahead.)*

Arrange 1 cookie on each of 8 plates. Using 4-inch heart-shaped cookie cutter, cut out 8 custard hearts. Place 1 custard heart atop each cookie. Spoon 2 tablespoons sauce over each heart. Set second cookie on top at slight angle. Spoon additional sauce alongside. Garnish with mint and serve.

## Be Mine Buttermilk Cake

*You're sure to win some hearts with this prize—a layer cake filled with Chambord truffle cream and topped with a chocolate glaze and raspberries.*

**8 servings**

### TRUFFLE CREAM

- 8 OUNCES BITTERSWEET (NOT UNSWEETENED) OR SEMISWEET CHOCOLATE, CHOPPED
- 1/3 CUP WHIPPING CREAM
- 2 TABLESPOONS (1/4 STICK) UNSALTED BUTTER, ROOM TEMPERATURE
- 1/4 CUP CHAMBORD OR OTHER BERRY LIQUEUR (SUCH AS CRÈME DE CASSIS)

### CAKE

- 1 3/4 CUPS ALL PURPOSE FLOUR
- 2 TEASPOONS BAKING POWDER
- 1/2 TEASPOON BAKING SODA
- 1/2 TEASPOON SALT
- 3/4 CUP SUGAR
- 1/2 CUP (1 STICK) UNSALTED BUTTER, ROOM TEMPERATURE
- 4 LARGE EGG YOLKS
- 1 CUP BUTTERMILK

### GLAZE

- 6 OUNCES BITTERSWEET (NOT UNSWEETENED) OR SEMISWEET CHOCOLATE, CHOPPED
- 1/4 CUP (1/2 STICK) UNSALTED BUTTER, CUT INTO SMALL PIECES
- 1/4 CUP LIGHT CORN SYRUP
- 1/4 CUP CHAMBORD OR OTHER BERRY LIQUEUR

FRESH RASPBERRIES OR STRAWBERRIES

**FOR TRUFFLE CREAM:** Stir chocolate, cream and butter in heavy medium saucepan over low heat until chocolate and butter melt and mixture is smooth. Mix in Chambord. Let stand at room temperature, stirring occasionally, about 2 hours.

**FOR CAKE:** Position rack in center of oven and preheat to 350°F. Butter 9-inch heart-shaped pan with 1 1/4-inch-high sides. Dust with flour; tap out excess. Sift first 4 ingredients into medium bowl. Using electric mixer at high speed, beat sugar and butter in large bowl until fluffy. Add yolks 1 at a time, beating just to combine after each addition. Using rubber spatula, mix in dry ingredients alternately with buttermilk, beginning and ending with dry ingredients.

Transfer batter to prepared pan. Bake cake until tester inserted into center comes out clean, about 35 minutes. Turn out cake onto rack and cool.

Cut cake horizontally in half. Place bottom layer on plate. Spread truffle cream over. Arrange top layer over and press gently to adhere. Using spatula, smooth cream on sides of cake if necessary. Chill until set, at least 1 hour.

**FOR GLAZE:** Stir chocolate and butter in heavy medium saucepan over low heat until melted and smooth. Remove from heat. Add corn syrup and liqueur and whisk until smooth. Let glaze stand until slightly thickened, stirring occasionally, about 30 minutes.

Place cake on rack set over baking sheet or large piece of foil. Pour glaze over cake, coating completely. Chill cake on rack until glaze is set, about 30 minutes. Transfer cake to platter. *(Can be made 1 day ahead. Cover with cake dome and chill. Bring to room temperature before serving.)* Garnish with berries.

ABOVE: WHITE-CHOCOLATE CUSTARD KISSING COOKIES.
BELOW: BE MINE BUTTERMILK CAKE.

## Valentine Lollipops

*Kids will love taking these treats (below) to school instead of giving the usual Valentine cards, and they can write their special messages on the ribbons. Two plastic lollipop molds, each containing six 2-inch heart-shaped depressions, are needed to make these candies. Imported milk chocolate can be used instead of bittersweet.*

### makes 12

SAFFLOWER OIL

2 PLASTIC 6-COUNT LOLLIPOP MOLDS*

8 OUNCES GOOD-QUALITY WHITE CHOCOLATE (SUCH AS LINDT OR BAKER'S), CHOPPED

8 OUNCES BITTERSWEET (NOT UNSWEETENED) OR SEMISWEET CHOCOLATE, CHOPPED

12 LOLLIPOP STICKS*

12 RED CELLOPHANE BAGS (OPTIONAL)*

12 GOLD RIBBONS (OPTIONAL)

Lightly oil lollipop molds. In small bowl set over saucepan of simmering water, stir white chocolate just until melted and smooth. Remove bowl from over water. In another small bowl set over same saucepan of simmering water, stir bittersweet chocolate just until melted and smooth. Cool both chocolates slightly.

Drizzle small spoonful of white chocolate into bottom of each mold. Drizzle small spoonful of bittersweet chocolate over. Using toothpick, swirl chocolates slightly to marbleize. Repeat layering of chocolates and swirling until molds are filled. Insert lollipop sticks into groove in molds and rotate sticks to coat with chocolate. Gently tap molds on work surface to release air bubbles. Refrigerate lollipops until very firm, at least 3 hours or overnight.

Refrigerate cookie sheets until chilled. Invert molds onto chilled cookie sheets. Gently bend corners to release lollipops (it may be necessary to let molds stand 30 seconds and then repeat bending). If desired, insert each lollipop into cellophane bag and tie decoratively with ribbon. *(Lollipops can be prepared 3 days ahead. Cover tightly and keep refrigerated.)*

*\*Available at candy supply stores.*

## Mousse-filled Chocolate Hearts

*Keep the hearts cold as you work with them to help prevent breakage.*

### 12 servings

HEARTS

10 OUNCES GOOD-QUALITY WHITE CHOCOLATE (SUCH AS LINDT OR BAKER'S), CHOPPED

8 OUNCES SEMISWEET CHOCOLATE, CHOPPED

MOUSSE

7 OUNCES SEMISWEET CHOCOLATE, CHOPPED

1 OUNCE UNSWEETENED CHOCOLATE, CHOPPED

3 TABLESPOONS UNSALTED BUTTER

⅓ CUP SUGAR

2 TABLESPOONS WATER

1 TABLESPOON LIGHT CORN SYRUP

2 LARGE EGG WHITES

⅛ TEASPOON CREAM OF TARTAR

½ CUP CHILLED WHIPPING CREAM

1 TEASPOON VANILLA EXTRACT

Turn two 15 x 10-inch baking sheets bottom side up. Dab butter on corners. Cover each pan bottom with parchment; press paper into butter.

Stir white chocolate in top of double boiler over barely simmering water until melted. Spread white chocolate over 1 sheet of parchment. Stir semisweet chocolate in clean top of double boiler over simmering water until melted. Spread semisweet chocolate over second sheet of parchment. Chill both sheets until chocolates are dry but still slightly flexible when edge of parchment is lifted, about 3 minutes for dark chocolate and 5 minutes for white chocolate (do not let harden).

Press heart-shaped cookie cutter about 3 inches long by 3 inches wide into chocolate, forming 12 hearts on each sheet (do not move or lift hearts). Chill until firm, about 30 minutes.

FOR MOUSSE: Combine both chocolates and butter in small saucepan. Stir over low heat until melted. Cool.

Combine sugar, 2 tablespoons water and corn syrup in heavy small saucepan. Stir over low heat until sugar dissolves. Increase heat; boil until candy thermometer registers 238°F, brushing down sides of pan with wet pastry brush, about 4 minutes.

Meanwhile, using electric mixer, beat egg whites and cream of tartar in large bowl until soft peaks form.

Gradually add boiling syrup to whites, beating until firm peaks form and meringue is completely cool, about 5 minutes. Gradually fold lukewarm chocolate mixture into meringue.

Beat cream and vanilla in small bowl until firm peaks form. Fold into chocolate mixture. Chill until cold, about 1 hour. (*Hearts and mousse can be made 1 day ahead. Keep chilled.*)

Turn 1 sheet of hearts out onto work surface. Peel off parchment. Cut around hearts, if necessary, to free from sheet of chocolate. Place on baking sheet and chill; transfer trimmings to small saucepan and reserve. Repeat cutting out hearts from second sheet, reserving trimmings in another pan.

Arrange 12 hearts on baking sheet. Spread ¼ cup of mousse over each, leaving ½-inch border. Top each with another chocolate heart. Refrigerate.

Using fork, stir dark chocolate trimmings over very low heat just until melted. Using another fork, stir white chocolate trimmings over very low heat just until melted. Dip tines of fork into dark chocolate; wave over hearts. Repeat with white chocolate. Chill 1 to 8 hours. Serve cold.

MOUSSE-FILLED CHOCOLATE HEARTS

# SAINT PATRICK'S DAY

IN THE CREATIVE DEVELOPMENT OF FLIMSY EXCUSES FOR THROWING A PARTY, WE NEED ALL YIELD TO THE IRISH AND THEIR BELOVED SAINT PATRICK'S DAY. CAN IT REALLY BE THAT THIS WILDLY POPULAR HOLIDAY (WHICH HAPPILY FALLS IN MARCH, A MONTH THAT FRANKLY REQUIRES A BIT OF CHEER) COMMEMORATES, BY SAINTLY EVICTION, THE RIDDING OF IRELAND OF ALL ITS SNAKES? FAITH AND BEGORRA, NOW THERE'S A GREAT REASON TO GATHER THE CLAN FOR A FINE OLD TIME!

SO DON YOUR GREEN APPAREL, INVITE YOUR LIVELIEST FRIENDS (EVEN IF THEY'RE NOT IRISH, AND HAVE A THING FOR REPTILES) AND BANISH THE GLOOM OF MARCH WITH THIS BONNY MEAL. LEAVING THE TRADITIONAL CORNED BEEF FOR ANOTHER YEAR, THIS UNEXPECTEDLY ELEGANT MENU FEATURES A RICH MEAT AND VEGETABLE STEW, A RIB-STICKING POTATO SIDE DISH AND AN HONEST, RUSTIC LOAF OF BREAD, ALL WASHED DOWN BY THE CLASSIC PUB BLEND OF LIGHT LAGER AND STOUT KNOWN AS A BLACK AND TAN. THINGS CONCLUDE WITH A BEAUTIFUL, NO-BLARNEY DESSERT. NOW AREN'T YOU GLAD YOU WOKE UP IRISH TODAY?

OPPOSITE (CLOCKWISE FROM TOP LEFT): COLCANNON; BEEF AND VEGETABLE STEW; AND SMOKED SALMON WITH BROWN SODA BREAD.

# SAINT PATRICK'S DAY DINNER *for* SIX

BLACK *and* TAN

SMOKED SALMON *with* BROWN SODA BREAD

BEEF *and* VEGETABLE STEW

COLCANNON

DOUBLE-CRUST LEMON TART *with* BERRIES

## Black and Tan

*If you have ever traveled anywhere in Ireland, you know that this beverage is served in virtually every pub in the country. Introduce it to your uninitiated friends at this celebration dinner.*

**6 servings**

3   12-OUNCE BOTTLES LIGHT LAGER
    (SUCH AS HARP), CHILLED
3   12-OUNCE BOTTLES GUINNESS
    STOUT, CHILLED

Halfway fill 6 beer mugs with lager. Pour Guinness stout over lager and serve drinks immediately.

## Smoked Salmon with Brown Soda Bread

*A plate of smoked salmon with brown soda bread is a calling card in Ireland. The greens and olive oil give a modern spin to this version of the classic starter.*

**6 servings**

3   CUPS TORN GREENS
    (SUCH AS RED LEAF LETTUCE,
    FRISÉE AND ARUGULA)
1   POUND THINLY SLICED SMOKED
    SALMON (SUCH AS IRISH,
    SCOTTISH OR NORWEGIAN)
2   TABLESPOONS DRAINED CAPERS
1   SMALL WHITE ONION,
    THINLY SLICED
24  RED CHERRY TOMATOES
    OR PEAR TOMATOES
24  YELLOW PEAR TOMATOES
    OR CHERRY TOMATOES
2   TABLESPOONS OLIVE OIL
    (PREFERABLY EXTRA-VIRGIN)
    LEMON WEDGES
    BROWN SODA BREAD
    (SEE RECIPE AT RIGHT)
    UNSALTED BUTTER

Divide greens among plates. Top with salmon. Sprinkle with capers. Garnish with onion and tomatoes. Drizzle with oil. Serve salmon with lemon wedges, bread and butter.

## Brown Soda Bread

**makes 1 loaf**

1    CUP PLUS 2 TABLESPOONS
     ALL PURPOSE FLOUR
4    CUPS WHOLE WHEAT FLOUR
⅓    CUP TOASTED WHEAT GERM
1½   TEASPOONS BAKING SODA
1½   TEASPOONS BAKING POWDER
1½   TEASPOONS SALT
2⅓   CUPS (ABOUT) BUTTERMILK

Preheat oven to 400°F. Sprinkle baking sheet with 2 tablespoons all purpose flour. Mix remaining 1 cup all purpose flour, 4 cups whole wheat flour, ⅓ cup toasted wheat germ, 1½ teaspoons baking soda, baking powder and salt in large bowl. Stir in enough buttermilk to form slightly moist dough. Turn bread dough out onto lightly floured work surface and knead dough until smooth, about 1 minute.

Pat dough into 8-inch round. Transfer dough round to prepared sheet. Using small sharp knife, cut ¼-inch-deep crisscross lines into top of dough round. Bake until bread sounds hollow when tapped on bottom, about 50 minutes. Transfer loaf to rack. Wrap loaf in towel. Cool bread completely.

## Beef and Vegetable Stew

*Since March 17 often falls on a weekday, this recipe was designed to be a good main course for an after-work party: You can make it ahead and reheat before serving.*

**6 servings**

3   TABLESPOONS VEGETABLE OIL

3   POUNDS BONELESS BEEF CHUCK, CUT INTO 1½-INCH CUBES

3   ONIONS, CHOPPED

1   12-OUNCE BOTTLE GUINNESS STOUT

2   CUPS (ABOUT) CANNED BEEF BROTH

1   POUND CARROTS, PEELED, CUT INTO 1½-INCH PIECES

1   POUND PARSNIPS, PEELED, CUT INTO 1½-INCH PIECES

1   POUND RUTABAGAS, PEELED, CUT INTO 1½-INCH PIECES

Heat 1 tablespoon oil in heavy large Dutch oven over high heat. Season beef with salt and pepper. Add ⅓ of beef to Dutch oven and brown well, about 5 minutes. Transfer beef to plate. Repeat with remaining 2 tablespoons oil and beef in 2 more batches. Reduce heat to medium. Add onions to Dutch oven and sauté until translucent, about 8 minutes. Return beef and any accumulated juices to Dutch oven. Add Guinness stout and enough broth to cover meat. Cover and bring to boil. Reduce heat and simmer until meat is almost tender, about 1 hour.

Add vegetables to stew and simmer uncovered until beef and vegetables are tender and gravy thickens slightly, stirring occasionally, about 1 hour. Season to taste with salt and pepper. *(Can be prepared 2 days ahead. Cover and chill. Rewarm over medium heat.)*

ABOVE: BROWN SODA BREAD WITH A BLACK AND TAN. BELOW: BEEF AND VEGETABLE STEW AND SMOKED SALMON.

## Colcannon

*A traditional dish that combines mashed potatoes, cooked cabbage and onions–Irish comfort food at its best.*

### 6 servings

4   POUNDS RUSSET POTATOES, PEELED, CUT INTO 1½-INCH PIECES

1   1½-POUND SAVOY CABBAGE, THINLY SLICED

1¼  CUPS WATER

1   CUP MILK

1   BUNCH GREEN ONIONS, CHOPPED

¾   CUP (1½ STICKS) UNSALTED BUTTER, ROOM TEMPERATURE

    CHOPPED FRESH CHIVES OR GREEN ONION TOPS

Cook potatoes in large pot of boiling salted water until tender. Drain. Return potatoes to pot and mash with potato masher. Set aside.

Combine cabbage and water in heavy large skillet. Boil until almost all liquid evaporates, tossing cabbage frequently, about 15 minutes. Mix cabbage into mashed potatoes.

Combine milk, green onions and ½ cup butter in heavy medium saucepan. Bring to boil, stirring to melt butter. Pour over potato mixture and stir to combine. Season to taste with salt and pepper. *(Can be prepared 2 hours ahead. Cover and let stand at room temperature. Before continuing, rewarm over low heat, stirring frequently.)* Mound mashed potatoes in bowl. Make well in center. Place remaining ¼ cup butter in well. Sprinkle with chives and serve.

## Double-Crust Lemon Tart with Berries

### 6 servings

#### FILLING

1   CUP SUGAR

⅔   CUP STRAINED FRESH LEMON JUICE

½   CUP (1 STICK) UNSALTED BUTTER, CUT INTO PIECES

3   TABLESPOONS GRATED LEMON PEEL

3   LARGE EGGS

#### CRUST

¼   CUP BLANCHED SLIVERED ALMONDS

1¾  CUPS ALL PURPOSE FLOUR

¼   CUP SUGAR

    PINCH OF SALT

10  TABLESPOONS (1¼ STICKS) UNSALTED BUTTER, ROOM TEMPERATURE

1   LARGE EGG

1   TABLESPOON MILK

1   TABLESPOON GRATED LEMON PEEL

1   TEASPOON VANILLA EXTRACT

1   EGG WHITE, BEATEN UNTIL FROTHY

    ADDITIONAL SUGAR

    WHIPPED CREAM

1   1-PINT BASKET STRAWBERRIES

1   ½-PINT BASKET RASPBERRIES

    FRESH MINT SPRIGS

FOR FILLING: Bring first 4 ingredients to boil in heavy large saucepan, stirring to dissolve sugar. Whisk eggs in medium bowl to blend. Gradually whisk in hot butter mixture. Return mixture to saucepan and stir over low heat until mixture thickens and leaves path on back of spoon when finger is drawn across, about 2 minutes; do not boil. Pour into bowl. Cover; chill overnight.

FOR CRUST: Finely grind almonds in processor. Transfer to bowl. Mix in flour, ¼ cup sugar and salt. Blend butter, 1 egg, milk, lemon peel and vanilla in processor until combined. Add dry ingredients and blend in using on/off turns until dough begins to come together. Turn dough out onto lightly floured surface and knead just until smooth. Divide dough into 2 unequal pieces that are ⅓ and ⅔ of entire amount. Flatten each piece into disk. Wrap in plastic and refrigerate at least 30 minutes. *(Can be prepared 1 day ahead. Let soften slightly at room temperature before rolling if necessary.)*

Preheat oven to 375°F. Roll out larger dough piece between sheets of waxed paper or plastic wrap to 12-inch round. Peel off top sheet of paper. Invert dough into 9-inch-diameter tart pan with removable bottom. Peel off top sheet of paper. Press dough onto bottom and up sides of pan, forming ½-inch high rim of pastry above pan. Crimp edge. Spoon cold filling into tart shell. Roll out smaller dough piece between sheets of waxed paper to 9½-inch round. Place atop filling in tart. Press dough top and sides together to seal. Fold crimped edge in. Press with fork tines to form decorative design.

Bake tart until top is brown, about 35 minutes. Transfer to rack and let stand 5 minutes. Brush top of tart with egg white; sprinkle with sugar. Bake 10 minutes more. Transfer tart to rack and cool completely. Remove tart pan sides. Transfer tart to platter. Cut into wedges. Top with whipped cream, berries and mint sprigs.

OPPOSITE: DOUBLE-CRUST LEMON TART WITH BERRIES.

**F**ORGET THE GREEN BEER.
IF YOU REALLY WANT TO
CELEBRATE WITH STYLE ON
SAINT PATRICK'S DAY, SERVE THIS
RICH CHOCOLATE MOUSSE CAKE.
ON THE INSIDE, CHOCOLATE MOUSSE
SPIKED WITH IRISH CREAM LIQUEUR
IS LAYERED WITH ESPRESSO SPONGE
CAKE THAT HAS BEEN SOAKED IN IRISH
WHISKEY SYRUP. ON THE OUTSIDE,
CHOCOLATE BANDS AND A MOUND OF
CHOCOLATE CURLS GIVE THIS CAKE A
STRAIGHT-FROM-THE-BAKERY LOOK—
ONE YOU CAN ACHIEVE AT HOME WITH
THE STEP-BY-STEP ADVICE HERE.

## *Irish Cream Chocolate Mousse Cake*

**12 servings**

### MOUSSE

| | |
|---|---|
| 4 | LARGE EGGS |
| ⅓ | CUP SUGAR |
| 12 | OUNCES SEMISWEET CHOCOLATE, CHOPPED |
| 1½ | CUPS CHILLED WHIPPING CREAM |
| ¼ | CUP IRISH CREAM LIQUEUR |

### CAKE

| | |
|---|---|
| 6 | LARGE EGGS |
| ¾ | CUP PLUS 2 TABLESPOONS SUGAR |
| 2 | TABLESPOONS INSTANT ESPRESSO POWDER |
| | PINCH OF SALT |
| 1 | CUP ALL PURPOSE FLOUR |

### SYRUP

| | |
|---|---|
| ⅔ | CUP SUGAR |
| 5 | TABLESPOONS WATER |
| 5 | TABLESPOONS IRISH WHISKEY |

### CHOCOLATE BANDS

| | |
|---|---|
| 2 | 14½ x 3-INCH WAXED PAPER STRIPS |
| 4 | OUNCES SEMISWEET CHOCOLATE, CHOPPED |
| 1 | TABLESPOON PLUS 1 TEASPOON SOLID VEGETABLE SHORTENING |

### CHOCOLATE CURLS

| | |
|---|---|
| 12 | 1-OUNCE SQUARES SEMISWEET BAKING CHOCOLATE |
| | POWDERED SUGAR |

**FOR MOUSSE:** Whisk eggs and sugar in large metal bowl. Set bowl over saucepan of simmering water (do not allow bottom of bowl to touch water) and whisk constantly until candy thermometer registers 160°F, about 5 minutes. Remove bowl from over water. Using electric mixer, beat egg mixture until cool and very thick, about 10 minutes.

Place chocolate in top of double boiler over simmering water; stir until melted and smooth. Remove chocolate from over water. Cool to lukewarm.

Combine cream and liqueur in medium bowl; beat to stiff peaks. Pour lukewarm melted chocolate over egg mixture and fold together. Fold in cream. Cover and chill until set, 4 hours or overnight.

**FOR CAKE:** Preheat oven to 350°F. Butter 9-inch-diameter springform pan with 2¾-inch-high sides. Line bottom with parchment paper. Using electric mixer, beat eggs, sugar, espresso powder and salt in large bowl until mixture thickens and slowly dissolving ribbon forms when beaters are lifted, about 8 minutes. Sift ⅓ of flour over and gently fold into egg mixture. Repeat 2 more times (do not overmix).

Pour batter into prepared pan. Bake until tester inserted into center comes out clean, about 35 minutes. Cool cake completely in pan on rack.

Run small sharp knife around pan sides to loosen cake. Release pan sides. Turn out cake. Remove pan bottom. Peel off parchment. *(Can be prepared 1 day ahead. Wrap cake in plastic and chill.)*

**FOR SYRUP:** Combine sugar and water in small saucepan. Stir over low heat until sugar dissolves. Increase heat and bring to boil. Remove from heat. Mix in whiskey. Cool.

Using serrated knife, cut cake horizontally into 3 layers. Place bottom cake layer on platter. Brush with 3 tablespoons syrup. Spread 2 cups mousse over. Top with second cake layer. Brush with 3 tablespoons syrup. Spread 2 cups mousse over. Top with third cake layer, cut side down. Brush with 3 tablespoons syrup. Spread remaining mousse over top and sides. Chill while preparing chocolate bands.

FOR CHOCOLATE BANDS: Line large baking sheet with foil and set aside. Place another large sheet of foil on work surface; top with waxed paper strips, spacing apart. Stir chopped semisweet chocolate and vegetable shortening in heavy small saucepan over low heat until melted and smooth. Pour half of melted chocolate down center of each waxed paper strip. Using metal icing spatula, spread chocolate to cover strips evenly and completely, allowing some chocolate to extend beyond edges of paper strips. Using fingertips, lift strips and place on clean foil-lined baking sheet. Refrigerate just until chocolate begins to set but is still very flexible, about 2 minutes.

Remove chocolate bands from refrigerator. Using fingertips, lift 1 band from foil. With chocolate side next to cake, place band around side of cake; press gently to adhere (band will be higher than cake). Repeat with second chocolate band, pressing onto uncovered side of cake so that ends of chocolate bands just meet (if ends overlap, use scissors to trim any excess paper and chocolate). Refrigerate until chocolate sets, about 5 minutes. Gently peel off paper. Refrigerate cake.

FOR CHOCOLATE CURLS: Line baking sheet with foil. Unwrap 1 square of chocolate. Place chocolate on its paper wrapper in microwave. Cook on high just until chocolate begins to soften slightly, about 1 minute (time will vary depending on power of microwave). Turn chocolate square onto 1 side and hold in hand. Working over foil-lined sheet, pull vegetable peeler along sides of chocolate, allowing chocolate curls to fall gently onto foil. Form as many curls as possible. Repeat process with remaining chocolate squares. Place curls atop cake, mounding slightly. (Can be prepared 1 day ahead. Chill.) Sift powdered sugar over curls.

1  FOR THE MOUSSE, WHISK EGGS AND SUGAR IN A BOWL OVER A PAN OF SIMMERING WATER UNTIL THE THERMOMETER REGISTERS 160°F. BE SURE TO WHISK CONSTANTLY SO THAT THE MIXTURE IS HEATED EVENLY.

2  NEXT, REMOVE THE EGG MIXTURE FROM OVER THE WATER AND BEAT UNTIL COOL AND THICK. POUR MELTED SEMISWEET CHOCOLATE OVER THE EGG MIXTURE AND USE A RUBBER SPATULA TO FOLD CHOCOLATE AND EGG TOGETHER.

3  FOR PROPER VOLUME IN THE CAKE BATTER, BEAT THE EGGS, SUGAR, ESPRESSO POWDER AND SALT IN A BOWL UNTIL MIXTURE THICKENS AND SLOWLY DISSOLVING RIBBON FORMS WHEN BEATERS ARE LIFTED.

4  TO CREATE THE CHOCOLATE BANDS, USE A METAL ICING SPATULA TO SPREAD THE MELTED CHOCOLATE MIXTURE OVER WAXED PAPER STRIPS. BE SURE TO COVER THE STRIPS EVENLY AND COMPLETELY.

5  USING YOUR FINGERTIPS, LIFT ONE CHILLED CHOCOLATE BAND WITH WAXED PAPER FROM FOIL. WITH THE CHOCOLATE SIDE NEXT TO CAKE, PLACE BAND AROUND ONE SIDE OF CAKE; PRESS GENTLY TO ADHERE. REPEAT WITH SECOND BAND.

6  FOR THE CHOCOLATE CURLS, TURN SOFTENED CHOCOLATE SQUARE ONTO ONE SIDE AND HOLD IN HAND. PULL VEGETABLE PEELER ALONG SIDES OF CHOCOLATE, ALLOWING CURLS TO FALL ONTO A FOIL-LINED SHEET.

# EASTER

Easter is one of the first spring holidays, and its religious message of rebirth is remarkably appropriate as the earth itself warms and awakens. Pastel pretty, with tulips and daffodils, bunnies and colored eggs among its decorations, Easter is both a spiritual holiday and a gently joyous one. As such, it can be celebrated in different ways. Here, we offer, among other treats, two parties: an elegant dinner of traditional Greek dishes and an easy brunch, designed to follow an Easter egg hunt.

The Greek meal centers around a succulent leg of lamb roasted with potatoes, artichokes and olives. Tangy dolmades, a shrimp soup and sautéed green beans round out the meal, with a luscious, strawberry-topped cheesecake-like pie for dessert. The brunch is a simple menu to serve once the Easter Bunny has come and gone, and the littlest egg hunters have checked every last hiding spot. The main course is a rich egg casserole that you can make ahead and pop in the oven while the hunt is on. Side dishes include a lovely salad and some crisp biscuits, while dessert makes the most of the season's new crop of berries.

# Greek Easter Feast *for* Eight

Pine Nut Dolmades *with*
Yogurt-Feta Dip

Shrimp Soup *with* Ouzo

Chilled Calliga Robula *or*
Sauvignon Blanc

Roast Leg *of* Lamb *with* Potatoes,
Artichokes *and* Olives

Green Beans Sautéed *with*
Red Bell Pepper Strips

Spring Green Salad

Zinfandel

Honey-Cheese Pie *with*
Strawberry Compote

Greek Coffee

Muscat

## Pine Nut Dolmades with Yogurt-Feta Dip

*A basket of crudités, including chilled steamed asparagus, yellow bell pepper strips, carrots, celery and cauliflower, is great before dinner with the dolmades and dip. You could also have* taramosalata *(fish roe spread), which can be purchased from a Greek market or restaurant. Partner it with pita bread triangles.*

**makes about 40**

1  14½-OUNCE CAN DICED TOMATOES IN JUICE

1  CUP LONG-GRAIN WHITE RICE

1  CUP THINLY SLICED GREEN ONIONS

½  CUP (PACKED) FINELY CHOPPED FRESH MINT (ABOUT 3 BUNCHES)

½  CUP (PACKED) FINELY CHOPPED FRESH DILL (ABOUT 4 BUNCHES)

½  CUP PINE NUTS, TOASTED

⅓  CUP EXTRA-VIRGIN OLIVE OIL

2  LARGE GARLIC CLOVES, MINCED

52  (ABOUT) GRAPE LEAVES FROM JAR (ABOUT TWO 2-POUND JARS)

¼  CUP FRESH LEMON JUICE

  YOGURT-FETA DIP (SEE RECIPE AT RIGHT)

Place tomatoes with their juice in large bowl. Add next 7 ingredients and mix to blend. Season with salt and pepper.

Rinse grape leaves under cold water. Drain. Cover bottom of heavy large Dutch oven with grape leaves (about 6). Place 1 grape leaf on work surface, vein side up; cut off stem. Place about 1 tablespoon rice mixture in center of leaf toward stem end. Fold sides over filling. Starting at stem end of leaf, roll up tightly as for egg roll. Place in Dutch oven, seam side down. Repeat with more leaves and rice mixture, layering dolmades when bottom of Dutch oven is covered.

Pour lemon juice over dolmades. Cover with grape leaves (about 6). Add enough water to pot so that dolmades are almost covered. Place heatproof plate atop dolmades to weigh down. Cover pot and bring to boil. Reduce heat to low; simmer until rice is tender and almost all liquid is absorbed, approximately 35 minutes.

Remove from heat; uncover. Allow dolmades to cool in pot. Drain any liquid remaining in pot. *(Can be prepared 2 days ahead. Cover and chill.)* Serve with Yogurt-Feta Dip.

## Yogurt-Feta Dip

**makes about 1½ cups**

1  CUP PLAIN YOGURT (DO NOT USE LOW-FAT OR NONFAT)

4  OUNCES FETA CHEESE, CRUMBLED

1  LARGE GREEN ONION, CUT INTO 1-INCH PIECES

¼  TEASPOON GRATED LEMON PEEL

Place all ingredients in processor and puree until almost smooth. Season with pepper. Chill until cold, at least 2 hours and up to 2 days.

## Shrimp Soup with Ouzo

*A rich lamb soup called* mageiritsa, *usually made with the leftover parts of the lamb, is always served at a Greek Easter dinner. As an alternative, try this light soup, filled with lots of Greek ingredients, including ouzo, the anise-flavored, brandy-based liqueur. Pour a Greek white wine such as Calliga Robula or a California Sauvignon Blanc.*

**8 servings**

12  CUPS WATER

2  POUNDS UNCOOKED LARGE SHRIMP, PEELED, DEVEINED, SHELLS RESERVED

4  TABLESPOONS OLIVE OIL

2  LARGE LEEKS (WHITE AND PALE GREEN PARTS ONLY), FINELY CHOPPED

2  CUPS FINELY CHOPPED TRIMMED FENNEL (ABOUT 2 MEDIUM BULBS)

1½  CUPS FINELY CHOPPED RED BELL PEPPER

⅓  CUP MINCED SHALLOTS

2½  CUPS CHOPPED SEEDED TOMATOES

3  LARGE GARLIC CLOVES, MINCED

1  CUP DRY WHITE WINE

¼  CUP OUZO (UNSWEETENED ANISE LIQUEUR) OR ANISETTE

  FENNEL FRONDS

Combine water and shrimp shells in heavy large pot (cover and refrigerate shrimp). Bring water with shells to boil. Reduce heat and simmer 20 minutes. Cover and remove from heat.

Heat 2 tablespoons oil in large Dutch oven over low heat. Add leeks, fennel, bell pepper and shallots. Cover and cook until vegetables are tender, stirring occasionally, about 30 minutes.

Uncover vegetables; add tomatoes and garlic and sauté until tomatoes soften and almost all liquid evaporates, about 8 minutes. Increase heat to medium. Add wine and boil 1 minute. Strain shrimp stock into vegetable mixture. Boil until mixture is reduced to 8 generous cups, about 1 hour 15 minutes.

Puree half of soup in blender in batches. Combine with remaining soup. Season with salt and pepper. *(Can be prepared 1 day ahead. Cover and refrigerate.)*

Season shrimp with salt and pepper. Heat 2 tablespoons oil in heavy large skillet over high heat. Add shrimp; sauté until cooked through, about 5 minutes. Add ouzo. Carefully ignite with lit match. Remove from heat; allow flames to subside. Ladle soup into bowls. Spoon some of shrimp and cooking liquid from skillet into each bowl. Garnish with fennel fronds.

OPPOSITE (CLOCKWISE FROM BOTTOM LEFT): PINE NUT DOLMADES; SPRING GREEN SALAD; SHRIMP SOUP WITH OUZO; AND ROAST LEG OF LAMB WITH POTATOES, ARTICHOKES AND OLIVES.

## Roast Leg of Lamb with Potatoes, Artichokes and Olives

*Roast spring lamb is the classic Greek Easter entrée. Round out the meal with green beans sautéed with red bell pepper, and tsoureki, a sweetened egg bread typical at Easter. (Look for it at a Greek market, or simply buy a braided egg bread at the bakery.) Uncork a Zinfandel. For a semi-boneless leg of lamb, ask a butcher to remove most of the large portion of the bone, leaving only the shank bone intact to hold the leg's shape.*

### 8 servings

- ½ CUP (PACKED) FRESH OREGANO LEAVES (ABOUT 3 BUNCHES)
- 8 LARGE GARLIC CLOVES
- 1 TABLESPOON COARSE SALT
- 1 TABLESPOON PEPPER
- 1 4-POUND SEMI-BONELESS LEG OF LAMB, FAT TRIMMED
- 4 TABLESPOONS OLIVE OIL

- 5 TABLESPOONS FRESH LEMON JUICE
- 4 MEDIUM ARTICHOKES, STEMS AND TOPS TRIMMED
- 1 LEMON, HALVED
- 24 BRINE-CURED BLACK OLIVES (SUCH AS KALAMATA)

- 6 8-OUNCE WHITE POTATOES, EACH CUT LENGTHWISE INTO 6 WEDGES

FRESH OREGANO SPRIGS

Finely mince ½ cup oregano, garlic, salt and pepper in processor. Place lamb in large roasting pan. Rub lamb with 2 tablespoons olive oil. Spread 4 tablespoons oregano mixture over lamb, reserving remainder. Arrange lamb so that fat side is up. Let stand at room temperature 1 hour.

Meanwhile, fill large pot with cold water. Add 4 tablespoons lemon juice to water. Cut 1 artichoke lengthwise into 8 wedges. Rub cut surfaces of artichoke with lemon half to prevent discoloring. Cut away choke and discard, leaving artichoke wedges intact. Place artichokes in pot with water. Repeat with remaining artichokes.

Boil artichokes until almost tender, about 15 minutes. Drain. Transfer to large bowl. Add olives, 1 tablespoon lemon juice and 1 teaspoon oregano mixture to artichokes; toss to coat.

Preheat oven to 450°F. Roast lamb for 10 minutes. Reduce oven temperature to 350°F.

Meanwhile, mix potatoes, 2 tablespoons oil and oregano mixture in bowl. Arrange potatoes around lamb in pan. Roast until thermometer inserted into thickest part of lamb registers 140°F, about 50 minutes.

Transfer lamb to large platter. Add artichoke mixture to roasting pan with potatoes; mix well. Continue roasting vegetables until tender, about 20 minutes. Surround lamb with vegetables. Garnish with oregano sprigs and carve roast at table.

## Spring Green Salad

*Here's a terrific version of one of the most popular salads in Greece.*

### 8 servings

- ½ CUP PLUS 1 TABLESPOON OLIVE OIL
- 6 TABLESPOONS FRESH LEMON JUICE
- 2 GARLIC CLOVES, PRESSED

- 16 CUPS TORN ROMAINE LETTUCE (ABOUT 1 LARGE HEAD)
- 1 ENGLISH HOTHOUSE CUCUMBER, CUT INTO 2½ x ¼ x ¼-INCH STRIPS
- 4 GREEN ONIONS, THINLY SLICED
- ¼ CUP MINCED FRESH DILL

Whisk oil, lemon juice and garlic in small bowl to blend. Season dressing with salt and pepper.

Combine lettuce, cucumber, green onions and dill in large bowl. Pour dressing over salad and toss to coat.

## Honey-Cheese Pie with Strawberry Compote

*This Easter dessert from the island of Siphnos is similar to cheesecake but not quite as rich. It traditionally contains ewe's-milk cheese, but this rendition uses ricotta and cream cheese; it's topped with honey-sweetened strawberries. Pass plates of assorted Greek cookies alongside, and offer demitasse cups of Greek coffee or espresso. You can also have sweet Muscat wine.*

### 12 servings

CRUST
- ¼ CUP (½ STICK) UNSALTED BUTTER
- 2 TABLESPOONS HONEY
- 35 VANILLA WAFER COOKIES
- ¾ CUP WHOLE ALMONDS
- ¾ CUP WALNUTS
- ¼ TEASPOON SALT

FILLING
- 2 8-OUNCE PACKAGES CREAM CHEESE, ROOM TEMPERATURE
- 1 15- TO 16-OUNCE CONTAINER WHOLE MILK RICOTTA CHEESE
- ½ CUP PLUS 1 TABLESPOON SUGAR
- ½ CUP PLUS 1 TABLESPOON HONEY
- 4 EXTRA-LARGE EGGS
- 2 TEASPOONS VANILLA EXTRACT
- ½ TEASPOON LEMON EXTRACT

COMPOTE
- 3 12-OUNCE BASKETS SMALL STRAWBERRIES, HULLED, QUARTERED
- ⅓ CUP HONEY

ADDITIONAL HONEY
STRAWBERRY BLOSSOMS OR OTHER SMALL NONPOISONOUS FLOWERS (OPTIONAL)

FOR CRUST: Preheat oven to 350°F. Wrap outside of 10-inch-diameter springform pan with 2½-inch-high sides with foil. Bring butter and honey to boil in heavy small saucepan, stirring occasionally. Remove from heat. Finely grind vanilla wafers in processor. Add nuts and salt to processor. Add butter mixture and process until nuts are finely chopped. Press mixture onto bottom and 1 inch up sides of prepared pan. Bake crust until golden, about 12 minutes. Transfer to rack and cool. Reduce oven temperature to 325°F.

FOR FILLING: Using electric mixer, beat cream cheese and ricotta cheese in large bowl until smooth. Mix in sugar and honey. Add eggs 1 at a time, beating well after each addition. Mix in extracts. Pour filling into crust.

Bake pie until puffed, golden and center moves only slightly when pan is gently shaken, about 1 hour 10 minutes. Transfer to rack and cool completely. *(Can be prepared 1 day ahead. Cover and refrigerate.)*

FOR COMPOTE: Mix quartered strawberries and ⅓ cup honey in large bowl. *(Can be made 4 hours ahead. Cover compote and refrigerate.)*

Run small sharp knife around sides of pan to loosen pie. Release pan sides. Drizzle additional honey over pie in zigzag pattern. Transfer pie to serving platter. Using slotted spoon, transfer some of strawberry compote to top of pie, if desired. Garnish pie with strawberry blossoms, if desired. Cut pie into wedges and serve with remaining strawberry compote.

HONEY-CHEESE PIE WITH STRAWBERRY COMPOTE

## EASTER EGG HUNT BRUNCH *for* EIGHT

ENDIVE *and* SNOW PEA SALAD

EGGS BAKED *with* LEEKS *and* TARRAGON

CRISP BISCUITS *with* HAM *and* ORANGE MARMALADE

CHARDONNAY, SAUVIGNON BLANC *or* ORANGE JUICE

MIXED BERRIES *with* CRÈME ANGLAISE *and* RASPBERRY SAUCE

ORANGE MADELEINES

## Endive and Snow Pea Salad

**8 servings**

- 3  TABLESPOONS RED WINE VINEGAR
- 2  TABLESPOONS DIJON MUSTARD
- ½  TEASPOON SALT
- ½  CUP PLUS 1 TABLESPOON OLIVE OIL
- 3  TABLESPOONS CHOPPED SHALLOTS

- 1  POUND SNOW PEAS, ENDS TRIMMED DIAGONALLY, STRINGS REMOVED
- 6  HEADS BELGIAN ENDIVE

Whisk vinegar, Dijon mustard and salt in small bowl. Gradually whisk in olive oil. Mix in shallots. Season with pepper. (*Can be prepared 2 hours ahead. Let stand at room temperature. Whisk dressing before using.*)

Blanch snow peas in large pot of boiling salted water 30 seconds. Drain. Refresh under cold water. Drain and pat dry. Transfer to large bowl.

Peel off outer leaves from Belgian endive and arrange in spoke fashion on large platter. Cut remaining endive into julienne. Add to snow peas. Add enough dressing to season to taste and toss well. Mound salad in center of endive-lined platter and serve.

## Eggs Baked with Leeks and Tarragon

*Save the hard-boiled eggs from the Easter egg hunt for another use. This recipe bakes fresh eggs into a rich main-course casserole. You can sauté the leeks and grate the cheeses ahead of time. Offer a chilled California Chardonnay or Sauvignon Blanc, with orange juice for the kids.*

**8 servings**

- 4  TABLESPOONS (½ STICK) UNSALTED BUTTER
- 3  LARGE LEEKS (WHITE AND PALE GREEN PARTS ONLY), COARSELY CHOPPED
- 1½  CUPS GRATED GRUYÈRE CHEESE (ABOUT 6 OUNCES)
- ½  CUP FRESHLY GRATED PARMESAN CHEESE (ABOUT 2 OUNCES)
- 8  LARGE EGGS
- 2  CUPS WHIPPING CREAM
- 2  TABLESPOONS PLUS 2 TEASPOONS CHOPPED FRESH TARRAGON OR 1½ TEASPOONS DRIED
- ½  TEASPOON SALT
- ¼  TEASPOON PEPPER
   FRESH TARRAGON SPRIGS

Preheat oven to 375°F. Butter 9 x 13-inch glass baking dish with 1 tablespoon butter. Melt remaining 3 tablespoons butter in heavy large skillet over medium-high heat. Add leeks and sauté until tender, about 5 minutes. Spread in bottom of prepared dish. (*Can be prepared 1 day ahead. Cover with plastic wrap and refrigerate.*)

Combine cheeses in bowl. Spread all but ½ cup cheese over leeks in dish. Whisk eggs, cream, chopped tarragon, salt and pepper in large bowl to blend. Pour into dish. Bake casserole until top is golden and center is set, about 30 minutes. Sprinkle remaining ½ cup cheese over. Bake until cheese melts, about 5 more minutes. Garnish with tarragon sprigs and serve.

## Crisp Biscuits with Ham and Orange Marmalade

*These buttermilk biscuits are baked until the bottoms are crisp. Filled with ham and marmalade, they are a great accompaniment to the baked egg casserole.*

**makes about 24**

- 2  CUPS ALL PURPOSE FLOUR
- 1  TABLESPOON SUGAR
- 2  TEASPOONS BAKING POWDER
- ½  TEASPOON BAKING SODA
- ½  TEASPOON SALT
- ¼  CUP CHILLED SOLID VEGETABLE SHORTENING, CUT INTO SMALL PIECES
- 2  TABLESPOONS (¼ STICK) CHILLED UNSALTED BUTTER, CUT INTO SMALL PIECES
- ¾  CUP (ABOUT) BUTTERMILK
- 1  EGG YOLK

- 3  TABLESPOONS UNSALTED BUTTER, MELTED
- ½  POUND COOKED HAM, SUCH AS HONEY BAKED, THINLY SLICED
- ¼  CUP ORANGE MARMALADE

Preheat oven to 425°F. Mix first 5 ingredients in large bowl. Add shortening and chilled butter and cut in until mixture resembles coarse meal. Make well in center. Add ½ cup buttermilk and egg yolk to well and stir until dough begins to come together, adding more buttermilk by tablespoons as necessary to form soft dough. Gather dough into ball. Turn dough out onto lightly floured surface and gently knead 30 seconds. Roll dough out to ⅜-inch-thick round. Cut into 2-inch rounds using cookie cutter. Gather scraps and reroll. Cut out additional rounds. Transfer to 2 heavy large cookie sheets. Bake biscuits until tops are golden brown and bottoms are crisp, about 15 minutes.

Cool biscuits slightly. Split in half horizontally. Brush insides with melted butter. Arrange ham over bottom halves, trimming to fit. Spread with marmalade. Assemble and serve.

OPPOSITE (CLOCKWISE FROM FAR LEFT): ENDIVE AND SNOW PEA SALAD; CRISP BISCUITS WITH HAM AND ORANGE MARMALADE; AND EGGS BAKED WITH LEEKS AND TARRAGON.

## Mixed Berries with Crème Anglaise and Raspberry Sauce

**8 servings**

RASPBERRY SAUCE

2    12-OUNCE BAGS FROZEN UNSWEETENED RASPBERRIES, THAWED

6    TABLESPOONS SUGAR

2    TABLESPOONS GRAND MARNIER OR OTHER ORANGE LIQUEUR

CRÈME ANGLAISE

2½   CUPS HALF AND HALF

1    VANILLA BEAN, SPLIT LENGTHWISE

6    EGG YOLKS

¾    CUP SUGAR

1½   TEASPOONS CORNSTARCH

2    TABLESPOONS COGNAC

8    CUPS MIXED ASSORTED BERRIES (SUCH AS BLACKBERRIES, RASPBERRIES, BLUEBERRIES AND HALVED HULLED STRAWBERRIES)

FRESH MINT SPRIGS

ORANGE MADELEINES (SEE RECIPE AT RIGHT)

**FOR RASPBERRY SAUCE:** Puree berries in processor. Strain through sieve, pressing on seeds. Mix sugar and Grand Marnier into puree. Cover and refrigerate until ready to use. *(Can be prepared 2 days ahead; keep refrigerated.)*

**FOR CREME ANGLAISE:** Place half and half in heavy medium saucepan. Scrape in seeds from vanilla bean; add bean. Bring to simmer. Whisk yolks, sugar and cornstarch in medium bowl to blend. Gradually whisk in hot half and half mixture. Return mixture to saucepan and stir over medium heat until custard thickens and leaves path on back of spoon when finger is drawn across, about 6 minutes. Strain into bowl. Mix in Cognac. Cover and refrigerate until well chilled. *(Can be prepared 2 days ahead; keep refrigerated.)*

Ladle both sauces simultaneously onto each plate. Mound berries in center. Garnish with mint sprigs. Serve with Orange Madeleines.

## Orange Madeleines

*The shell-shaped pans for making these cookies (below with the Mixed Berries with Crème Anglaise and Raspberry Sauce) are available at cookware shops.*

**makes about 24**

3    LARGE EGGS

2    LARGE EGG YOLKS

⅔    CUP SUGAR

1    TABLESPOON MINCED ORANGE PEEL (ORANGE PART ONLY)

1    TEASPOON VANILLA EXTRACT

½    TEASPOON ORANGE EXTRACT

¼    TEASPOON SALT

1    CUP SIFTED ALL PURPOSE FLOUR

¼    CUP (½ STICK) UNSALTED BUTTER, MELTED, COOLED TO LUKEWARM

POWDERED SUGAR

Preheat oven to 375°F. Butter and flour madeleine pans. Using electric mixer, beat first 7 ingredients in large bowl until pale yellow and almost tripled in volume, about 6 minutes. Sift flour over; fold in gently but thoroughly; do not overwork or batter will deflate. Pour butter into small bowl. Fold in ¼ cup batter. Quickly fold butter mixture back into remaining batter. Spoon batter into prepared pans, filling almost to top. Bake until golden, about 10 minutes. Cool 1 minute in pans. Using small sharp knife, gently remove madeleines from pans. Cool. *(Can be made 1 day ahead. Store airtight at room temperature.)* Sift powdered sugar over and serve.

# *An* EASTER HAM *and* ITS LEFTOVERS

THOSE WHO ARE STICKLERS FOR TRADITION MAY NOT THINK AN EASTER BUFFET COMPLETE WITHOUT A HAM. SO FOR THAT REASON, WE'VE INCLUDED ONE HERE, A DELICIOUS BAKED HAM THAT GETS SLICED, TOPPED WITH A MUSTARD-ACCENTED APPLE CIDER SAUCE AND THEN REWARMED. AND BECAUSE A HAM VIRTUALLY GUARANTEES LEFTOVERS, WE'VE ALSO INCLUDED TWO RECIPES—A MAIN COURSE SALAD AND A PASTA—THAT MAKE THE MOST OF WHAT REMAINS.

## Baked Ham with Cider Sauce

### 8 servings

- 1 5- TO 6-POUND BONE-IN WATER-ADDED HAM, BUTT PORTION
- 3 CUPS APPLE CIDER
- 1½ CUPS PACKED DRIED APPLE CHUNKS (ABOUT 4½ OUNCES)
- ¾ CUP PACKED GOLDEN BROWN SUGAR
- 6 TABLESPOONS CIDER VINEGAR
- 3 TABLESPOONS DIJON MUSTARD

Preheat oven to 325°F. Place ham in roasting pan and bake until thermometer inserted into thickest part of ham registers 150°F, about 15 minutes per pound. Cool ham completely. *(Can be prepared 3 days ahead. Cover and chill.)*

Bring cider and apples to boil in heavy medium saucepan over medium-high heat. Boil until liquid is reduced to scant 1½ cups, about 8 minutes. Whisk sugar, vinegar and mustard in small bowl until blended. Add to cider mixture. Simmer until reduced to 2¼ cups, stirring occasionally, about 6 minutes. *(Can be made 1 day ahead.)*

Preheat oven to 375°F. Cut eight ½-inch-thick ham slices from bone. Overlap ham slices in glass baking dish. Spoon sauce over. Bake until ham is heated through and sauce bubbles, about 25 minutes. Transfer to platter.

## Layered Ham and Vegetable Salad

### 2 servings

- ⅓ CUP LOW-FAT MAYONNAISE
- ⅓ CUP NONFAT SOUR CREAM
- 1 TEASPOON WORCESTERSHIRE SAUCE
- ½ TEASPOON HOT PEPPER SAUCE (SUCH AS TABASCO)
- ¼ CUP CRUMBLED BLUE CHEESE

- 1 POUND SUPERMARKET SALAD BAR INGREDIENTS (PACKED SEPARATELY), INCLUDING AT LEAST 4 VEGETABLES (SUCH AS LETTUCE, SPINACH, SHREDDED CARROTS, SHREDDED RED CABBAGE, PEAS AND SLICED MUSHROOMS)
- 1 CUP DICED HAM
- 4 CHERRY TOMATOES, HALVED CHOPPED NUTS (OPTIONAL)

Whisk first 4 ingredients in small bowl to blend. Mix in blue cheese. Season dressing to taste with salt and pepper.

In 6-cup soufflé dish (preferably clear glass), alternate layers of salad bar ingredients and ham. Spread dressing over; arrange cherry tomato halves and nuts, if desired, atop dressing. Serve immediately or chill up to 8 hours.

## Penne with Ham and Vegetables

### 2 servings

- 1½ TABLESPOONS OLIVE OIL
- 1 CUP DICED HAM
- 1 SMALL RED BELL PEPPER, COARSELY CHOPPED
- ½ CUP CHOPPED ONION
- ½ TEASPOON DRIED THYME
- 2 TABLESPOONS DIJON MUSTARD
- ¾ CUP HALF AND HALF
- 1 CUP FROZEN PETITE PEAS, THAWED
- ½ CUP GRATED PARMESAN CHEESE
- 6 OUNCES PENNE, FRESHLY COOKED

Heat olive oil in heavy medium skillet over medium-high heat. Add diced ham, chopped bell pepper, chopped onion and thyme and sauté until vegetables are soft and ham begins to brown, about 6 minutes. Mix in mustard. Add half and half, peas, Parmesan cheese and pasta. Simmer until sauce reduces slightly and coats pasta, stirring occasionally, 5 minutes. Season with salt and pepper and serve.

# HOW *to* MAKE CHOCOLATE EASTER EGGS

T HERE ARE EASTER EGGS,
COLORED, DYED, STICKERED
AND WRAPPED, AND THEN
THERE ARE THESE EASTER EGGS:
ARTFUL, MOLDED CHOCOLATE CONCOC-
TIONS, EVERY BIT AS DELICIOUS TO
EAT AS THEY ARE BEAUTIFUL TO LOOK
AT. THEY MAKE A LOVELY CENTERPIECE
AND SWEET TREAT AT THE END OF
YOUR EASTER MEAL. JUST DON'T LET
THE RABBIT HIDE THEM.

## Chocolate-Caramel Easter Eggs

*It's important to use an imported choco-
late, such as Lindt, for this recipe. The
high cocoa-butter content of the imported
type produces chocolate eggs that are
flexible and easy to unmold.*

**makes 3 large eggs
and 4 small eggs**

### EGGSHELLS

2½ POUNDS IMPORTED BITTERSWEET
(NOT UNSWEETENED) CHOCOLATE
OR IMPORTED WHITE
CHOCOLATE (SUCH AS LINDT)
OR 1¼ POUNDS OF EACH
CHOCOLATE, CHOPPED

3 LARGE PLASTIC EGG MOLD SETS*
(TOTAL OF SIX 4¼ X 3-INCH
½-CUP EGG HALVES)

2 SMALL PLASTIC EGG MOLD SETS*
(TOTAL OF EIGHT 3 X 2½-INCH
¼-CUP EGG HALVES)

### CARAMEL FILLING

3 CUPS SUGAR

¾ CUP WATER

½ CUP WHIPPING CREAM

½ CUP (1 STICK) UNSALTED BUTTER

⅓ CUP SOUR CREAM

### CHOCOLATE FILLING

¾ CUP WHIPPING CREAM

6 TABLESPOONS (¾ STICK)
UNSALTED BUTTER, CUT
INTO PIECES

1 POUND IMPORTED BITTERSWEET
(NOT UNSWEETENED)
CHOCOLATE, CHOPPED

6 TABLESPOONS SOUR CREAM

### DECORATIONS

8 YARDS (ABOUT) SILK RIBBONS

FOR EGGSHELLS: Line cookie sheet
with aluminum foil. Melt chocolate in
top of double boiler over simmering
water, stirring frequently until smooth
and candy thermometer registers 115°F
for bittersweet and 105°F for white
chocolate. (If making both bittersweet
chocolate and white chocolate eggs,
melt chocolates separately in 2 double
boilers.) Remove chocolate from over
water. Spoon chocolate into 1 set of
large molds, filling molds completely
(do not fill decorative base section
of mold). Turn mold over above prepared cookie sheet, allowing excess
chocolate to spill out. Shake mold to
produce uniformly thick shell. Turn
mold right side up. Run fingertip
gently around edge of eggs to remove
excess chocolate. Refrigerate.

Tilt foil-lined sheet with melted chocolate over top of double boiler, scraping
chocolate into double boiler. Reheat to
115°F for bittersweet and 105°F for
white chocolate, stirring frequently.
Repeat coating process with remaining
2 large egg mold sets and 2 small egg
mold sets, removing from over water
while working and reheating chocolate
after each set of egg molds is coated.
Refrigerate molds. (If using white
chocolate, the molds will need a double coating. Refrigerate molds after
first coating is cold. Refill with barely
lukewarm chocolate, shake out excess
and wipe edges clean, creating double-
thick shell.) Return remaining chocolate on foil to top of double boiler.

FOR CARAMEL FILLING: Stir sugar and
water in heavy large saucepan over low
heat until sugar dissolves. Increase heat
and boil without stirring until syrup
turns deep amber, washing down sides
of pan with pastry brush dipped into
water and swirling pan occasionally.
Remove from heat. Add whipping cream
and butter and whisk until smooth.
Whisk in sour cream. Let caramel filling
stand just until barely cool, stirring
occasionally, about 50 minutes.

Spoon 2 scant tablespoons caramel into each small egg half. Spoon ¼ cup caramel into each large egg half. Chill.

FOR CHOCOLATE FILLING: Bring whipping cream and butter to simmer in heavy medium saucepan, stirring until butter melts. Add chocolate and whisk until smooth and melted. Remove filling from heat. Whisk in sour cream. Let stand until cool but still pourable, stirring occasionally, 30 minutes.

Spoon filling over caramel in all egg halves, filling to 1/16 inch below top edge. Chill until set, about 40 minutes.

Rewarm reserved chocolate in double boiler to 115°F for bittersweet and 105°F for white chocolate. Remove from over water. Working quickly, spread enough melted chocolate (use bittersweet for dark eggs and white chocolate for white eggs) atop 1 set of filled eggs just to cover. Use icing spatula to scrape excess chocolate from eggs and clean sides. Place mold in refrigerator. Repeat with remaining egg molds. Refrigerate until firm, about 1 hour.

Line cookie sheets with aluminum foil. Remove 1 egg mold from refrigerator. Turn mold over onto foil. Gently bend and twist mold side to side several times to release halves. Repeat.

Rewarm remaining melted chocolate in top of double boiler until warm to touch. Turn bottom half of 1 egg over so flat side faces up. Spread small amount of melted chocolate over flat side of egg, leaving ¼-inch border. Working quickly, cover bottom half of egg with corresponding top half of egg and press together gently. Refrigerate whole egg. Repeat with remaining egg halves and melted chocolate. *(Can be prepared 2 weeks ahead. Refrigerate.)*

FOR DECORATION: Wrap ribbons around seam of each egg and tie bow at top. Refrigerate until ready to eat.

*Available at candy supply stores.

**1** LARGE CHOCOLATE EGGSHELLS ARE MADE BY POURING MELTED WHITE CHOCOLATE INTO THE BOTTOM AND TOP HALVES OF MOLDS, FILLING COMPLETELY.

**2** THE MOLD IS TILTED TO RELEASE THE EXCESS CHOCOLATE SO THAT A HOLLOW SHELL IS FORMED. USE YOUR FINGERTIP TO WIPE AWAY THE EXCESS CHOCOLATE.

**3** THE CARAMEL FILLING IS SPOONED INTO CHOCOLATE EGGSHELL HALVES. AFTER THE CARAMEL SETS, IT IS COVERED WITH DARK CHOCOLATE FILLING.

**4** MELTED WHITE CHOCOLATE IS SPREAD OVER DARK CHOCOLATE FILLING IN EACH EGG HALF, COVERING COMPLETELY.

**5** AFTER WHITE CHOCOLATE IS SET, MOLD IS TURNED OVER, THEN GENTLY BENT AND TWISTED TO RELEASE EGG HALVES.

**6** WHITE CHOCOLATE IS SPREAD OVER FLAT SIDE OF BOTTOM EGG HALF; THEN TOP EGG HALF IS PLACED OVER BOTTOM EGG HALF AND PRESSED GENTLY TO ADHERE.

# PASSOVER

Like Easter, Passover is an ancient religious observation closely associated with food. Symbolically based on historical events from the Bible, the eight days of the Passover celebration are centered around the meal known as the seder, and commemorate the Jewish exodus from slavery in Egypt. Matzo, the thin, unleavened cracker-like bread, is the most potent symbol of the holiday, representing the loaves that the fleeing Jews, pressed for time, were forced to bake without rising. Now leavenings are prohibited during Passover. This restriction can be something of a challenge to the cook, but never a bar to eating joyously and well, while remaining deeply in touch with the past.

Here is a modern Passover seder menu that is, nevertheless, steeped in Jewish tradition. It concludes with a deliciously indulgent unleavened cake (one among several others that appear in the pages that follow) that utterly redefines the notion of "dietary restriction"—unless, of course, you're thinking about having a second piece.

Opposite (clockwise from top left): Golden Gratin; Baked Whitefish with Dill and Tomato-Cucumber Relish; Rosemary Rib Roast; and Red Wine Mushroom Ragout.

## Chicken Soup with Miniature Leek-Chive Matzo Balls

*For bigger matzo balls, form the mixture into 12 rounds and cook them for one hour ten minutes. The matzo balls can be prepared ahead, a fact that makes this soup (below) ideal for entertaining.*

**12 servings**

| | |
|---|---|
| 6 | TABLESPOONS (¾ STICK) UNSALTED PAREVE MARGARINE* |
| ½ | CUP PACKED FINELY CHOPPED LEEK (WHITE AND PALE GREEN PARTS ONLY) |
| ½ | CUP FINELY CHOPPED FRESH CHIVES |
| 4 | EGGS |
| 2 | TABLESPOONS GINGER ALE |
| 1½ | TEASPOONS COARSE KOSHER SALT |
| ¼ | TEASPOON PEPPER |
| ¼ | TEASPOON GROUND GINGER |
| 1 | CUP UNSALTED MATZO MEAL |
| 12 | CUPS CHICKEN BROTH CHOPPED FRESH CHIVES |

Melt margarine in heavy small skillet over medium heat. Add leek; sauté 5 minutes. Remove from heat. Add ½ cup chives.

Beat eggs, ginger ale, salt, pepper and ginger to blend in bowl. Mix in matzo meal and leek mixture. Cover and chill until firm, at least 2 hours.

Line large baking sheet with plastic wrap. Using moistened palms, roll rounded teaspoons of matzo mixture into balls. Place on prepared baking sheet. Chill 30 minutes.

Bring large pot of salted water to boil. Drop in matzo balls; cover pot. Cook matzo balls until tender and evenly colored throughout, about 40 minutes. Using slotted spoon, transfer matzo balls to bowl. *(Can be made 3 days ahead. Cover and chill.)*

Bring chicken broth to simmer in large pot. Add matzo balls and cook until warmed through, about 10 minutes.

Place 4 matzo balls in each of 12 bowls. Ladle soup over. Garnish with chives.

*\*A nondairy margarine available at most supermarkets across the country.*

## Baked Whitefish with Dill and Tomato-Cucumber Relish

*A delicious alternative to gefilte fish. Have the fishmonger fillet the whitefish.*

**12 servings**

FISH

VEGETABLE OIL

1   4- TO 4¼-POUND WHITEFISH, CUT INTO 2 FILLETS, FATTY PORTIONS TRIMMED ALONG CENTER AND FLAP EDGES

3   CUPS COARSELY CHOPPED FRESH DILL (ABOUT SIX ½-OUNCE PACKAGES)

1   MEDIUM ONION, COARSELY CHOPPED

1   TEASPOON COARSE KOSHER SALT

¼   TEASPOON PEPPER

6   TABLESPOONS WHITE VINEGAR

RELISH

4   CUPS DICED PEELED SEEDED CUCUMBER (ABOUT 4)

2   POUNDS PLUM TOMATOES (ABOUT 12 LARGE), SEEDED, CHOPPED

½   CUP CHOPPED FRESH DILL

¼   CUP WHITE VINEGAR

4   TEASPOONS COARSE KOSHER SALT

FRESH DILL SPRIGS

FOR FISH: Line heavy baking sheet with foil; brush with oil. Arrange fish skin side down on foil. Finely chop dill and onion in processor. Sprinkle each fillet with half of salt and pepper. Press dill mixture firmly over. Pour vinegar evenly over. Cover and chill overnight, basting occasionally with juices.

Position rack in center of oven and preheat to 375°F. Uncover fish and bake until just cooked through, about 25 minutes. Let stand at room temperature 30 minutes. Cover and chill at least 2 hours and up to 2 days.

FOR RELISH: Combine first 5 ingredients in medium bowl. Let stand 3 hours, stirring occasionally. Season relish with pepper.

Scrape most of dill off fish. Cut crosswise into 12 portions; trim neatly. Slide spatula under each, separating from skin. Arrange fish on plates. Drain relish and spoon over fish. Garnish with dill sprigs.

## Rosemary Rib Roast

*An impressive centerpiece dish. This looks beautiful when surrounded with sautéed baby vegetables. Start marinating the meat one day ahead. Serve homemade or purchased horseradish alongside.*

**12 servings**

½   CUP CHOPPED FRESH ROSEMARY (ABOUT FIVE ½-OUNCE PACKAGES)

6   TABLESPOONS VEGETABLE OIL

8   LARGE GARLIC CLOVES, CHOPPED

2   TEASPOONS COARSE KOSHER SALT

1   7- TO 7½-POUND WELL-TRIMMED BONELESS BEEF RIB ROAST, TIED

RED WINE MUSHROOM RAGOUT (SEE RECIPE AT RIGHT)

FRESH ROSEMARY SPRIGS

Grind chopped rosemary, oil, garlic and salt in processor to chunky paste. Place beef in roasting pan. Rub rosemary mixture all over beef. Cover and refrigerate for 1 day.

Position rack in center of oven and preheat to 350°F. Uncover beef and roast until thermometer inserted straight down from top center registers 125°F for rare, about 1 hour 45 minutes. Let stand 30 minutes. Transfer roast to platter. Scrape pan drippings into cup; spoon off fat. Add juices to Red Wine Mushroom Ragout (see recipe).

Garnish roast with rosemary sprigs. Serve with mushroom ragout.

## Red Wine Mushroom Ragout

**12 servings**

¼   CUP VEGETABLE OIL

5   POUNDS MEATY BEEF NECK BONES, CUT INTO 2-INCH PIECES

1   POUND ONIONS, SLICED

7   CUPS WATER

2   750-ML BOTTLES DRY RED WINE

1   LARGE PLUM TOMATO, CHOPPED

⅛   TEASPOON GROUND CLOVES

¼   CUP (½ STICK) UNSALTED PAREVE MARGARINE*

1   CUP CHOPPED SHALLOTS

1   LARGE FRESH ROSEMARY SPRIG

3   POUNDS MUSHROOMS, THICKLY SLICED

DEGREASED PAN JUICES FROM ROSEMARY RIB ROAST (SEE RECIPE AT LEFT; OPTIONAL)

Heat oil in heavy large pot over high heat. Add bones and onions and cook until brown, turning mixture over and scraping bottom of pot frequently, about 25 minutes. Add 1 cup water and boil until reduced to glaze, scraping bottom frequently, about 8 minutes. Add remaining 6 cups water, wine, tomato and cloves. Bring to boil. Reduce heat and simmer 4 hours. Strain stock into bowl, pressing on solids. Chill at least 1 hour. *(Can be made 4 days ahead.)*

Remove fat from surface of stock. Boil stock in medium saucepan until reduced to 2 cups, about 30 minutes.

Melt margarine in heavy 14-inch skillet or Dutch oven over high heat. Add chopped shallots and rosemary and sauté 2 minutes. Add sliced mushrooms and cook until juices are released, stirring frequently, about 10 minutes. Add stock and boil until sauce coats spoon lightly, about 15 minutes. Season to taste with salt and pepper. *(Can be made 3 days ahead. Refrigerate. Rewarm ragout over low heat.)* Add degreased pan juices from roast if desired.

*\*A nondairy margarine available at most supermarkets across the country.*

There is an injunction against using fermented or leavened grains, called *chometz*, during Passover. These include wheat, barley, rye, oats and spelt (an ancient grain). Any food or beverage derived from such grains is also considered chometz. In place of flour, cake meal made from ground matzo is often used.

In addition, Jews of Eastern European origin (the Ashkenazim) refrain from eating a group of foods known as *kitniyot*. This is a legacy of religious authorities who believed it was necessary to take every precaution against using chometz, and prohibited certain foods because of their similarity to grains. These include anything made from corn, beans, peas, lentils, rice, kasha, peanuts and soy products.

Naturally, such restrictions affect what can be baked for Passover. There are many common baking ingredients that are kosher, yet still not permitted during this holiday. Flour, baking powder and yeast are chief among them, but there are less obvious ones that cannot be used: cornstarch and corn syrup, which are derived from corn; powdered sugar, which contains cornstarch; alcoholic beverages made from grain; vanilla extract, because it contains grain alcohol; brown sugar, which may contain yeast; and certain oils.

## Golden Gratin

*This not-too-sweet potato dish is reminiscent of tzimmes, a traditional sweet potato, carrot and short rib stew. Using a four-millimeter slicing blade in the processor makes the preparation a snap.*

### 12 servings

| | |
|---|---|
| 4 | CUPS PASSOVER APRICOT NECTAR* |
| 1 | CUP CANNED CHICKEN BROTH |
| 6 | TABLESPOONS (¾ STICK) UNSALTED PAREVE MARGARINE* |
| ½ | CUP CHOPPED DRIED APRICOTS |
| 1½ | TEASPOONS COARSE KOSHER SALT |
| ½ | TEASPOON GROUND CINNAMON |
| ½ | TEASPOON PEPPER |
| 5½ | POUNDS LONG ORANGE-FLESHED YAMS, PEELED, SLICED ⅛ INCH THICK |

Position rack in center of oven and preheat to 400°F. Generously grease 13 x 9 x 2-inch glass baking dish.

Stir nectar, broth, 6 tablespoons margarine, apricots, salt, cinnamon and pepper in heavy large pot over high heat until margarine melts. Add sliced yams; bring to boil. Cover pot; cook until yams begin to soften, stirring often, about 15 minutes.

Using slotted spoon, transfer yams to prepared dish. Pour juices from pot over; press firmly to compact. Cover dish with heavy foil. Bake 30 minutes. Uncover and bake yams until tender and beginning to brown on top, about 55 minutes. Let stand 15 minutes.

*\*Available at kosher stores and many supermarkets across the country.*

## Chocolate, Orange and Honey Cake

*Two layers of tender orange sponge cake are embellished with a rich orange and honey chocolate glaze. Any leftover chocolate glaze can be chilled, rolled into small rounds and kept refrigerated to serve as truffles with coffee or tea.*

### 12 servings

CAKE

| | |
|---|---|
| 7 | LARGE EGGS, SEPARATED |
| ½ | TEASPOON COARSE KOSHER SALT |
| 1 | CUP SUGAR |
| ⅓ | CUP VEGETABLE OIL |
| ¼ | CUP FROZEN ORANGE JUICE CONCENTRATE, THAWED |
| 3 | TABLESPOONS GRATED ORANGE PEEL |
| ¼ | TEASPOON FRESH LEMON JUICE |
| ¾ | CUP MATZO CAKE MEAL |
| 5 | TABLESPOONS POTATO STARCH |

GLAZE

| | |
|---|---|
| ¾ | CUP (1½ STICKS) UNSALTED PAREVE MARGARINE* |
| 1½ | POUNDS BITTERSWEET (NOT UNSWEETENED) OR SEMISWEET CHOCOLATE, CHOPPED |
| 1 | CUP PLUS 2 TABLESPOONS FROZEN ORANGE JUICE CONCENTRATE, THAWED |
| 3 | TABLESPOONS HONEY |

NONPOISONOUS FLOWERS (OPTIONAL)

ORANGE PEEL STRIPS (OPTIONAL)

FOR CAKE: Position rack in center of oven and preheat to 350°F. Line bottom of 10-inch-diameter springform pan with foil; brush foil with oil. Cut cardboard into 9-inch round. Wrap with foil. Set aside.

Using electric mixer, beat egg whites and salt in large bowl until soft peaks form. Gradually add ½ cup sugar and beat until stiff glossy peaks form.

In another large bowl, beat egg yolks, remaining ½ cup sugar, vegetable oil, orange juice concentrate, orange peel and lemon juice until blended. Sift cake meal and potato starch over yolk mixture and beat at low speed just until blended. Gently fold whites into yolk mixture in 2 additions.

Transfer batter to prepared pan. Bake cake until tester inserted into center comes out clean, about 45 minutes. Cool cake in pan on rack. *(Can be prepared 1 day ahead. Cover and let stand at room temperature.)*

FOR GLAZE: Melt margarine in heavy large saucepan over low heat. Add chopped chocolate and stir until melted and smooth. Mix in orange juice concentrate and honey. Let glaze cool until thickened but still spreadable, about 2 hours.

Cut around pan sides to loosen cake. Release sides. Cut cake in half horizontally, leaving cake bottom on pan bottom. Place top half of cake, top side down, on foil-wrapped cardboard round. Spread 1⅓ cups chocolate glaze over. Place bottom half of cake, pan side up, onto glaze. Remove pan bottom; peel off foil. Spread 1 cup chocolate glaze in thin layer over entire cake, anchoring crumbs. Refrigerate cake for 30 minutes.

Rewarm remaining chocolate glaze over very low heat until just pourable. Place rack on baking sheet; place cake on rack. Pour glaze over cake, coating entirely and smoothing sides with metal spatula. Chill cake on rack until glaze is firm. Transfer to platter. (Reserve glaze on sheet for another use.) *(Can be made 3 days ahead. Cover and chill. Let stand at room temperature 1 hour before serving.)*

Garnish cake with flowers and orange peel strips if desired.

*A nondairy margarine available at most supermarkets across the country.*

CHOCOLATE, ORANGE AND HONEY CAKE

# HOW *to* MAKE *a* PASSOVER LAYER CAKE

EVERY SPRING, FAMILIES AND FRIENDS ALL OVER THE WORLD GATHER TO CELEBRATE PASSOVER, THE ANCIENT JEWISH HOLIDAY THAT IS SO RICH IN TRADITION. WHEN THE SEDER MEAL IS FINISHED, IT'S IMPORTANT TO HAVE A DESSERT EVERY BIT AS SPECIAL AS THE HOLIDAY ITSELF. HERE'S ONE THAT IS IMPRESSIVE, DELICIOUS—AND FULLY WITHIN THE GUIDELINES OF PASSOVER BAKING.

## Almond and Hazelnut Torte with Raspberry Filling

**12 servings**

### CAKE

UNSALTED PAREVE MARGARINE*
MATZO CAKE MEAL

| | |
|---|---|
| 2 | CUPS BLANCHED ALMONDS, TOASTED |
| 2 | CUPS HAZELNUTS, TOASTED |
| ¼ | CUP PLUS 3 TABLESPOONS UNSWEETENED COCOA POWDER |
| 1 | TEASPOON GROUND CINNAMON |
| ¼ | TEASPOON GROUND NUTMEG |
| 10 | LARGE EGGS, SEPARATED |
| 1¾ | CUPS SUGAR |
| ¼ | TEASPOON SALT |
| 1 | TEASPOON FRESH LEMON JUICE |
| 3 | OUNCES BITTERSWEET (NOT UNSWEETENED) OR SEMISWEET CHOCOLATE, CHOPPED |

### FROSTING

| | |
|---|---|
| 1½ | CUPS SUGAR |
| 1 | 4-INCH-LONG PIECE VANILLA BEAN, CUT INTO 4 PIECES |
| 4 | LARGE EGG WHITES |
| ⅓ | CUP WATER |
| 1 | TEASPOON FRESH LEMON JUICE |
| | PINCH OF SALT |
| ½ | CUP SEEDLESS RASPBERRY JAM |
| | FRESH STRAWBERRIES, HALVED |

**FOR CAKE:** Preheat oven to 350°F. Grease three 9-inch-diameter cake pans with 2-inch-high sides with unsalted margarine. Line with parchment. Grease parchment. Dust pans with matzo cake meal; shake out excess. Combine almonds, hazelnuts, ¼ cup unsweetened cocoa powder, ground cinnamon and nutmeg in processor and process until most of nuts are finely ground (do not overprocess or mixture will form paste).

Using electric mixer, beat egg yolks with 1¼ cups sugar in large bowl until pale yellow and slowly dissolving ribbon forms when beaters are lifted, about 4 minutes. Using electric mixer fitted with clean dry beaters, beat egg whites and salt in another large bowl until very soft peaks form. Beat in lemon juice. Gradually add remaining ½ cup sugar; beat until stiff but not dry. Fold half of ground-nut mixture into yolk mixture. Fold in ⅓ of egg whites. Fold in chopped bittersweet chocolate and remaining nut mixture. Fold in remaining beaten egg whites in 2 batches.

Divide batter among prepared pans. Smooth tops. Bake until tester inserted into center comes out clean, about 35 minutes. Run small sharp knife around cake pan sides. Cool cakes in pans on racks 5 minutes.

Line racks with paper towels; sprinkle with remaining 3 tablespoons cocoa powder. Turn out cakes onto cocoa-dusted towels. Peel off parchment paper. Cool cakes completely. *(Can be prepared 1 day ahead. Cover cakes with plastic wrap; let cakes stand at room temperature.)*

FOR FROSTING: Blend sugar and vanilla in processor until very finely chopped, stopping occasionally to scrape down sides of bowl, about 2 minutes. Strain through sieve to remove any large pieces of vanilla. Transfer sugar to large bowl. Add egg whites, water, lemon juice and salt to sugar; whisk to blend.

Set bowl over saucepan of simmering water (do not allow bowl to touch water). Using electric mixer, beat mixture over medium-low heat until candy thermometer registers 140°F, about 8 minutes. Continue cooking 3 minutes, beating constantly (mixture will resemble marshmallow creme). Remove bowl from over water and continue beating frosting until cool and thick, about 8 minutes.

Melt jam in heavy small saucepan over low heat, stirring frequently. Place 1 cake layer on platter. Tuck 4 strips of waxed paper under cake to keep platter clean. Spread ¼ cup jam atop cake. Cover with 1 cup frosting. Top with second cake layer. Spread remaining jam atop cake. Cover with 1 cup frosting. Top with third cake layer. Spread remaining frosting in thick swirls over top and sides of cake. *(Can be prepared 1 day ahead. Cover with cake dome and let stand at room temperature.)*

Arrange berries atop cake.

*\*A nondairy margarine available at most supermarkets across the country.*

**1** TO BEGIN THE CAKE, GRIND NUTS, COCOA AND SPICES IN PROCESSOR JUST UNTIL MOST OF THE NUTS ARE FINELY GROUND. DO NOT OVERPROCESS, OR THE NUTS WILL RELEASE OILS AND THE MIXTURE WILL FORM A PASTE.

**2** NEXT, BEAT YOLKS AND SUGAR UNTIL THEY ARE PALE YELLOW AND A SLOWLY DISSOLVING RIBBON FORMS WHEN THE BEATERS ARE LIFTED FROM THE BOWL.

**3** FOLD HALF OF THE GROUND-NUT MIXTURE INTO YOLK MIXTURE; THEN FOLD IN ONE-THIRD OF THE BEATEN EGG WHITES TO LIGHTEN THE BATTER.

**4** FOR THE FROSTING, BEAT EGG WHITES, SUGAR, WATER, LEMON JUICE AND SALT IN A BOWL SET OVER A SAUCEPAN OF SIMMERING WATER UNTIL THE MIXTURE REGISTERS 140°F. CONTINUE COOKING FOR THREE MINUTES.

**5** AFTER LAYERING THE CAKE WITH SOME OF THE FROSTING, SPREAD THE REMAINDER IN THICK SWIRLS OVER THE TOP AND SIDES OF THE CAKE.

# MORE DELICIOUS PASSOVER DESSERTS

**D**URING THE EIGHT DAYS OF PASSOVER, THERE ARE STRICT PROHIBITIONS AGAINST FOODS WITH LEAVENING OR YEAST. IN PLACE OF BREAD, MATZO, AN UNLEAVENED CRACKER-LIKE FOOD, IS PERMITTED. OTHER BAKED GOODS, ALSO UNLEAVENED, ARE MADE WITH THE FLOUR AND MEAL FROM GROUND MATZO.

THESE RESTRICTIONS DON'T HAVE TO MAKE IT DIFFICULT TO SERVE A DELICIOUS DESSERT AT PASSOVER, AS THESE FIVE RECIPES PROVE. THEY COMBINE FRESH AND DRIED FRUITS, A VAREITY OF NUTS, SPICES AND CHOCOLATE, AND THEY RANGE FROM HOMESPUN TO ELEGANT. PICK THE ONE THAT SUITS YOUR SEDER.

## Trio of Sorbets with Raspberry Coulis

*Refreshing in looks and taste, these light fruit sorbets (below left) served in a colorful raspberry sauce are perfect after a filling seder meal.*

**8 servings**

BANANA SORBET

1½  POUNDS RIPE BANANAS (ABOUT 4 MEDIUM-LARGE)
⅔  CUP SUGAR
½  CUP WATER
2  EGG YOLKS
1  TABLESPOON PLUS 1 TEASPOON FRESH LEMON JUICE
   PINCH OF SALT
   PINCH OF GROUND GINGER

APRICOT SORBET

2  CUPS WATER
1  CUP SUGAR

1  6-OUNCE PACKAGE DRIED APRICOTS
½  CUP DRY WHITE WINE
⅛  TEASPOON GROUND GINGER
   PINCH OF SALT

KIWI SORBET

1  CUP SUGAR
½  CUP WATER

2  POUNDS KIWIS (ABOUT 9 LARGE), PEELED, DICED

   RASPBERRY COULIS (SEE RECIPE OPPOSITE)
   FRESH BANANA SLICES, KIWI SLICES AND RASPBERRIES (OPTIONAL)

**FOR BANANA SORBET:** Place bananas in freezer to chill 10 minutes. Bring sugar and ½ cup water to simmer in heavy small saucepan over medium heat, stirring until sugar dissolves. Beat egg yolks in small bowl to blend. Gradually whisk hot syrup into yolks. Return mixture to same saucepan and stir over low heat just until bubbles appear at pan edge and mixture thickens slightly, stirring constantly, about 2 minutes. Pour yolk mixture into processor. Add fresh lemon juice, salt and ground ginger. Peel cold bananas and slice. Add to processor bowl. Puree until smooth. Immediately transfer custard to ice cream maker and freeze according to manufacturer's instructions. Transfer to container and freeze. *(Sorbet can be prepared 2 days ahead. Store in freezer.)*

FOR APRICOT SORBET: Bring 1 cup water and 1 cup sugar to boil in heavy small saucepan over medium heat, stirring until sugar dissolves. Pour into processor bowl and cool.

Combine remaining 1 cup of water, apricots and wine in heavy medium saucepan. Cover and cook over medium-low heat until apricots are very tender, stirring occasionally, about 25 minutes. Add mixture to syrup in processor. Add ginger and salt and puree. Cool apricot mixture.

Transfer apricot mixture to ice cream maker and freeze according to manufacturer's instructions. Transfer sorbet to container and freeze. *(Can be prepared 2 days ahead. Store in freezer.)*

FOR KIWI SORBET: Bring sugar and ½ cup water to boil in heavy small saucepan over medium heat, stirring until sugar dissolves. Cool.

Puree diced kiwi in processor. Set aside 1 cup puree. Strain remaining puree through fine sieve. Combine both purees and syrup in ice cream maker and freeze according to manufacturer's instructions. Transfer to container and freeze. *(Sorbet can be prepared 2 days ahead. Store in freezer.)*

Spread Raspberry Coulis in center of each dessert plate. Arrange 1 scoop of each sorbet on sauce. Garnish with fresh fruit if desired and serve.

## Raspberry Coulis

**makes about 2⅔ cups**

| | |
|---|---|
| 2 | 12-OUNCE BAGS FROZEN UNSWEETENED RASPBERRIES, THAWED |
| ½ | CUP SUGAR |
| ¼ | CUP RASPBERRY JAM |

Puree all ingredients in processor. Strain through fine sieve. *(Can be prepared 2 days ahead. Cover and chill.)*

## Raisin Streusel Cake

*Make this homespun dessert (below right) up to two days ahead.*

**12 servings**

STREUSEL

| | |
|---|---|
| ¼ | CUP (½ STICK) UNSALTED MARGARINE, ROOM TEMPERATURE |
| ⅔ | CUP SUGAR |
| 4¼ | TEASPOONS GROUND CARDAMOM |
| 2¼ | TEASPOONS GROUND CINNAMON |
| ½ | CUP MATZO CAKE MEAL |

CAKE

| | |
|---|---|
| ½ | CUP MATZO CAKE MEAL |
| ½ | CUP POTATO STARCH |
| ½ | TEASPOON SALT |
| ½ | TEASPOON GROUND GINGER |
| 5 | LARGE EGG WHITES, ROOM TEMPERATURE |
| 1⅓ | CUPS SUGAR |
| 5 | LARGE EGG YOLKS |
| ⅓ | CUP LIQUID NONDAIRY CREAMER |
| ¼ | CUP (½ STICK) UNSALTED MARGARINE, MELTED, COOLED |
| 2 | TABLESPOONS GRATED LEMON PEEL |
| 1½ | TABLESPOONS FRESH LEMON JUICE |
| ⅔ | CUP RAISINS |

FOR STREUSEL: Position rack in center of oven and preheat to 350°F. Coat 9 x 9-inch pan with 2-inch-high sides generously with margarine. Mix ¼ cup margarine, sugar and spices in medium bowl. Gradually add matzo meal and mix until crumbly. Spread half of streusel on baking sheet and bake until golden and crisp, about 10 minutes. Cool and break into bits.

FOR CAKE: Combine first 4 ingredients in small bowl. Using electric mixer, beat egg whites in large bowl until soft peaks form. Gradually add 1 cup sugar and beat until stiff but not dry.

Using same beaters, beat egg yolks and remaining ⅓ cup sugar in another bowl until mixture is thick and slowly dissolving ribbon forms when beaters are lifted. At low speed, beat in nondairy creamer, then margarine, lemon peel and lemon juice. Add dry ingredients and stir until well blended. Fold in egg whites in 2 additions.

Pour half of batter into prepared pan. Sprinkle baked streusel over. Sprinkle with half of raisins. Spread remaining cake batter over. Sprinkle with unbaked streusel and remaining raisins. Bake until tester inserted into center of cake comes out dry, about 40 minutes. Cool cake in pan on rack. Cover with foil and let stand 1 hour to soften topping. *(Can be prepared 2 days ahead. Keep covered and store at room temperature.)* Cut into squares and serve.

# CINCO DE MAYO

WHEN IT COMES TO HOLIDAYS, MEXICO SEEMS TO HAVE MORE THAN ITS FAIR SHARE. WHETHER THIS IS BECAUSE THE PEOPLE OF MEXICO REALLY KNOW HOW TO HAVE A GOOD TIME, OR WHETHER THEY HAVE SUCH A GOOD TIME BECAUSE THEY HAVE SO MANY HOLIDAYS REMAINS A MYSTERY. ALSO A MYSTERY IS HOW THE U.S. HAS COME TO CELEBRATE CINCO DE MAYO, A HOLIDAY THAT COMMEMORATES THE DAY IN 1862 WHEN THE MEXICANS SUCCESSFULLY OPPOSED AN INVASION OF THEIR COUNTRY BY THE FRENCH. SOMEBODY SOMEWHERE CO-OPTED THE HOLIDAY, THINKING IT A FINE EXCUSE FOR THROWING A PARTY ON THIS SIDE OF THE BORDER. WHICH, IN THE OPEN SPIRIT OF THE NORTH AMERICAN FREE TRADE AGREEMENT, IS EXACTLY WHAT WE HAVE DONE.

SINCE CINCO DE MAYO COMES FREE OF ANY HIDEBOUND CULINARY TRADITIONS, OUR MENU RUNS THE SOUTH-OF-THE-BORDER GAMUT. IT GETS STARTED WITH A NEW TWIST ON THE MARGARITA, INCLUDES AN ASSORTMENT OF RIB-STICKING AND SLIGHTLY FIERY MAINS AND SIDES, AND ENDS WITH A PAIR OF LUSCIOUS DESSERTS. AND AS CREATIVE AS THESE OFFERINGS ARE, THEY ARE REL-ATIVELY SIMPLE TO MAKE AND DON'T REQUIRE ANY HARD-TO-FIND INGREDIENTS. TO COMPLETE THE GOOD TIMES, JUST ADD A PIÑATA, A STICK AND BLINDFOLD.

OPPOSITE (CLOCKWISE FROM TOP LEFT): FROZEN MARGARITAS; CHILAQUILES; AND POZOLE.

# MOTHER'S DAY

A national day to honor mothers seems like such a natural idea that it's surprising to learn that a number of influential women campaigned for years before President Woodrow Wilson was given the power to proclaim it as such in 1914, and then did so the following year. And while we have no proof of this, we firmly believe that the corsage was invented the next day, and that restaurants for the first time in history opened on Sunday for brunch.

Nowadays, Mother's Day is one of the busiest—if not *the* busiest—days of the year for restaurants across the country. In the interest of avoiding crowds and cold food, consider staying home and celebrating she who usually does all the cooking by cooking up something wonderful just for her. This can be as elaborate as a festive Champagne brunch or as simple—yet luscious—as homemade sticky buns served to Mom in bed, on a tray adorned with a single, perfect rose. And if you really want to make her day, don't forget to do the dishes once you're done cooking.

Opposite: Creamy Smoked Salmon and Dill Tart; Wild Mushroom and Bell Pepper Sauté; and Belgian Endive and Grapefruit Salad.

## Frozen Boysenberry and White Chocolate Parfait

*Begin preparing this delicious dessert at least one day ahead.*

**6 servings**

PARFAIT

1   16-OUNCE BAG FROZEN BOYSENBERRIES OR BLACKBERRIES, THAWED
¼   CUP SUGAR
1   TABLESPOON CRÈME DE CASSIS OR OTHER BERRY-FLAVORED LIQUEUR
½   TEASPOON FRESH LEMON JUICE

¾   CUP SUGAR
¼   CUP WATER
6   LARGE EGG YOLKS
3   OUNCES GOOD-QUALITY WHITE CHOCOLATE (SUCH AS LINDT OR BAKER'S), CHOPPED, MELTED
2   TEASPOONS VANILLA EXTRACT
1⅔  CUPS CHILLED WHIPPING CREAM

SAUCE

1   16-OUNCE BAG FROZEN BOYSENBERRIES OR BLACKBERRIES, THAWED
¼   CUP SUGAR
2   TABLESPOONS CRÈME DE CASSIS OR OTHER BERRY-FLAVORED LIQUEUR

FRESH BOYSENBERRIES, BLACKBERRIES OR STRAWBERRIES
FRESH MINT SPRIGS

FOR PARFAIT: Line 9 x 5-inch loaf pan with plastic wrap. Puree berries and ¼ cup sugar in blender until just smooth. Strain. Measure 1⅓ cups puree and place in heavy small saucepan. (Reserve any remaining puree for sauce.) Simmer 1⅓ cups puree over medium heat until reduced to scant 1 cup, stirring occasionally, about 8 minutes. Transfer to bowl and chill 30 minutes. Stir in crème de cassis and lemon juice. Refrigerate reduced puree until ready to use.

Combine ¾ cup sugar, water and yolks in medium metal bowl. Set bowl over saucepan of simmering water. Using hand-held electric mixer, beat yolk mixture until it registers 140°F on candy thermometer, occasionally scraping down sides of bowl, about 5 minutes. Continue cooking 3 minutes, beating constantly. Remove from over water. Add warm melted chocolate and vanilla extract and beat until cool. Beat whipping cream in another large bowl to stiff peaks. Gently mix ¼ of whipped cream into chocolate mixture. Fold in remaining whipped cream.

Transfer 1⅓ cups chocolate mixture to medium bowl. Fold in reduced berry puree. Fill prepared loaf pan with ⅓ of remaining chocolate mixture. Cover with berry-chocolate mixture. Top with remaining chocolate mixture. Smooth top. Freeze parfait overnight. *(Can be prepared 2 days ahead.)*

FOR SAUCE: Puree frozen boysenberries, sugar and crème de cassis in blender or processor until smooth. Strain. Add any extra berry puree reserved from parfait.

Unmold frozen parfait. Peel off plastic wrap. Slice into ½-inch-thick slices. Drizzle with sauce. Garnish with berries and fresh mint sprigs.

## Coffee Wafers

*Cream cheese enriches the dough for these cookies, which are extremely easy to make. They would be nice with the parfait.*

**makes about 2 dozen**

2   TABLESPOONS INSTANT COFFEE CRYSTALS
1   TABLESPOON WHIPPING CREAM
2   TEASPOONS VANILLA EXTRACT
1   EGG YOLK
½   CUP (1 STICK) UNSALTED BUTTER, ROOM TEMPERATURE
2   OUNCES CREAM CHEESE, ROOM TEMPERATURE
1¼  CUPS POWDERED SUGAR
1   TABLESPOON GOLDEN BROWN SUGAR
1¾  CUPS ALL PURPOSE FLOUR
½   TEASPOON SALT
½   TEASPOON BAKING POWDER
⅓   CUP DRIED CURRANTS

ADDITIONAL POWDERED SUGAR

Preheat oven to 350°F. Line 2 heavy large baking sheets with aluminum foil. Stir coffee, whipping cream and vanilla extract in large bowl until coffee dissolves. Mix in egg yolk. Add butter and cream cheese. Using electric mixer, beat mixture until smooth. Add 1¼ cups powdered sugar and brown sugar. Beat until well blended. Sift flour, salt and baking powder into butter mixture. Add dried currants; mix until just blended. Refrigerate dough until just firm, about 15 minutes.

Roll 1 tablespoon dough into ball. Roll ball in additional powdered sugar to coat thickly. Place on prepared sheet. Press with fingertips to form 2½- to 3-inch round. Repeat with remaining dough, spacing rounds 1 inch apart on prepared sheets.

Bake cookies until golden brown on bottom, about 15 minutes. Cool on rack. *(Can be prepared 1 day ahead. Store in airtight container.)*

## Maple-Pecan Sticky Buns

**makes 12**

### DOUGH

| | |
|---|---|
| ¼ | CUP WARM WATER (105°F TO 115°F) |
| 1 | ENVELOPE DRY YEAST |
| ⅓ | CUP OLD-FASHIONED OATS |
| ⅓ | CUP SUGAR |
| 3 | TABLESPOONS UNSALTED BUTTER, CUT INTO PIECES |
| 2 | TEASPOONS GRATED LEMON PEEL |
| 1½ | TEASPOONS SALT |
| 1¼ | CUPS MILK (DO NOT USE LOW-FAT OR NONFAT) |
| 1 | LARGE EGG |
| 1 | LARGE EGG YOLK |
| 2 | TEASPOONS VANILLA EXTRACT |
| 4½ | CUPS (ABOUT) UNBLEACHED ALL PURPOSE FLOUR |

VEGETABLE OIL

### SYRUP

| | |
|---|---|
| 1 | CUP PURE MAPLE SYRUP |
| 9 | TABLESPOONS (1 STICK PLUS 1 TABLESPOON) UNSALTED BUTTER |
| 1 | CUP FIRMLY PACKED GOLDEN BROWN SUGAR |
| ½ | CUP PECANS, COARSELY CHOPPED |

### FILLING

| | |
|---|---|
| ¾ | CUP PECANS |
| ½ | CUP FIRMLY PACKED GOLDEN BROWN SUGAR |
| ½ | CUP RAISINS |
| 2 | TEASPOONS GROUND CINNAMON |
| 3 | TABLESPOONS UNSALTED BUTTER, MELTED |

WHAT MOM WOULDN'T APPRECIATE SLEEPING LATE ON HER BIG DAY, FOLLOWED BY BREAKFAST IN BED? AND TO MAKE THE MEAL REALLY SPECIAL, ADD THESE IRRESISTIBLE STICKY BUNS TO HER TRAY, ALONG WITH FLOWERS, SOME FRUIT, THE PAPER AND A CUP OF COFFEE. THEY'RE MADE WITH A HIGH-RISING YEAST DOUGH, WHICH GETS ROLLED UP WITH A FILLING OF PECANS, RAISINS AND CINNAMON. THE BUNS ARE BAKED IN A WONDERFUL "STICKY" MAPLE-SYRUP GLAZE FOR AN EXTRA DOSE OF DELICIOUSNESS.

**FOR DOUGH:** Place water in small bowl. Sprinkle yeast over and stir to blend. Let stand until yeast dissolves, about 8 minutes.

Combine oats, ⅓ cup sugar, butter, lemon peel and salt in large bowl. Heat milk in small saucepan until bubbles form around edge of pan. Pour hot milk over oat mixture and stir until butter melts and sugar dissolves. Cool to 105°F to 115°F, about 10 minutes.

Add egg, egg yolk, vanilla and dissolved yeast to oat mixture; stir to blend. Mix in 3 cups flour. Using firm rubber spatula or large wooden spoon, beat batter 100 strokes. Cover bowl with plastic wrap; let batter rest in bowl for 10 minutes.

Using spatula, mix enough flour into batter, ¼ cupful at a time, to form soft dough. Turn dough out onto floured surface. Knead gently until smooth and slightly sticky dough forms, adding more flour if dough is very sticky, about 8 minutes.

Lightly oil large bowl. Place dough in bowl; turn to coat with oil. Cover bowl with plastic wrap, then with towel. Let dough rise in warm draft-free area until doubled in volume, about 1½ hours. Meanwhile, prepare syrup and filling.

**FOR SYRUP:** Butter two 13 x 9 x 2-inch glass baking dishes. Combine maple syrup and butter in heavy medium skillet. Stir over medium heat until butter melts. Remove from heat. Mix in brown sugar. Pour half of syrup into each prepared dish; tilt to coat bottom of dishes evenly. Sprinkle each with half of chopped nuts; cool.

FOR FILLING: Combine all ingredients in processor. Using on/off turns, blend until pecans are finely chopped. Transfer mixture to bowl.

Carefully turn doubled dough out onto floured surface (do not punch down dough). Roll dough gently to flatten slightly. Using hands, pull and stretch dough to 12 x 18-inch rectangle. Brush dough with all of melted butter. Sprinkle filling evenly over dough, leaving ½-inch plain border on 1 long side. Starting at long side opposite uncovered border, roll up dough jelly roll style, forming log. Pinch seam to seal. Using heavy large knife, score log into 12 equal pieces. Cut log at scores. Arrange 6 pieces, cut side up and evenly spaced, in each prepared baking dish. Lightly press down on buns with palm of hand. Cover pans tightly with plastic wrap. *(Can be prepared 1 day ahead. Refrigerate overnight.)*

Let buns rise in warm draft-free area until light and puffy, about 50 minutes if buns are at room temperature or 1 hour 15 minutes if refrigerated.

Position rack in center of oven and preheat to 375°F. Bake buns uncovered until tops are golden brown and syrup bubbles thickly, reversing position of dishes halfway through baking time, about 25 minutes.

Remove baking dishes from oven. Immediately place large baking sheet over 1 baking dish. Using oven mitts as aid, grasp dish and baking sheet together and turn over, releasing buns and topping onto sheet. Turn second dish of buns out onto another baking sheet. Cool buns 5 minutes. *(Can be made ahead. Cool buns completely. Wrap buns tightly with foil on baking sheet. Freeze up to 2 weeks. Bake frozen buns covered at 375°F until heated through, about 15 minutes.)* Serve buns hot.

1   PREPARE A BATTER THAT INCLUDES FLOUR, SUGAR, OATS, MILK AND YEAST; BEAT FOR ONE HUNDRED STROKES WITH A FIRM RUBBER SPATULA. COVER AND SET ASIDE FOR TEN MINUTES. THEN MIX IN ENOUGH FLOUR, 1/4 CUPFUL AT A TIME, TO FORM A SOFT DOUGH.

2   TURN THE DOUGH OUT ONTO A FLOURED SURFACE AND KNEAD GENTLY. IF THE DOUGH IS VERY STICKY, ADD MORE FLOUR, AND CONTINUE KNEADING UNTIL THE DOUGH IS SMOOTH AND ONLY SLIGHTLY STICKY.

3   TRANSFER THE DOUGH TO A GREASED BOWL; ALLOW THE DOUGH TO RISE IN A WARM, DRAFT-FREE AREA UNTIL DOUBLED IN VOLUME. ONCE IT HAS RISEN SUFFICIENTLY, THE DOUGH WILL RETAIN INDENTATIONS WHEN PRESSED.

4   AFTER THE DOUGH HAS RISEN, GENTLY ROLL IT OUT ON A LIGHTLY FLOURED SURFACE. PULL AND STRETCH TO SHAPE DOUGH INTO A 12 x 18-INCH RECTANGLE.

5   BRUSH THE DOUGH WITH MELTED BUTTER, AND SPRINKLE THE FILLING OVER. FROM ONE LONG SIDE, ROLL UP THE DOUGH TO ENCLOSE THE FILLING AND FORM A LOG.

6   TO CREATE 12 BUNS OF THE SAME SIZE, SCORE THE DOUGH LOG 11 TIMES; THEN USE A SHARP KNIFE TO CUT THROUGH THE LOG AT THE MARKS.

# MEMORIAL DAY

A TIME TO REMEMBER FALLEN HEROES AND OTHERS WHO HAVE PASSED ON, MEMORIAL DAY REMAINS A SOLEMN CELEBRATION FOR SOME. MORE RECENTLY, IT HAS ALSO COME TO MARK THE FIRST LONG WEEKEND OF SUMMER, THOUGH THE SEASON ITSELF IS STILL SEVERAL WEEKS OFF BY THE CALENDAR. SCHOOL'S OUT (OR ALMOST—THINGS SEEMED TO HAVE CHANGED SINCE WE WERE RATHER YOUNGER), AND, DEPENDING ON WHERE YOU LIVE, THE HOLIDAY CAN COINCIDE WITH THE FIRST REALLY WARM DAYS OF THE YEAR, MAKING IT AN IDEAL EXCUSE FOR A PICNIC.

WHETHER HEADED FOR THE BEACH OR SIMPLY A LAWN CHAIR UNDER A SHADE TREE IN THE BACK YARD, KICKING OFF THE LAID-BACK SEASON BY LABORING IN THE KITCHEN MAKES NO SENSE AT ALL. THAT'S WHY THE TWO EASY, DO-AHEAD PICNIC MENUS HERE CONCENTRATE ON FLAVORFUL, PORTABLE AND OTHERWISE COOL-TO-SERVE CUISINE. ONE INCLUDES TUNA SALAD SANDWICHES ENLIVENED WITH CAPERS, OLIVE PASTE AND ARUGULA, WHILE THE OTHER FEATURES A BEAUTIFUL ROASTED CHICKEN AND BELL PEPPER SALAD. SIMPLE SIDE DISHES AND PACKABLE DESSERTS ROUND THINGS OUT, LEAVING ONLY THE WEATHER TO CHANCE.

## MEMORIAL DAY BEACH PICNIC *for* SIX

MEDITERRANEAN OLIVES *and* CORNICHONS

SALADE NIÇOISE SANDWICHES

GREEN BEAN SALAD *with* BASIL VINAIGRETTE

ROSÉ *or* BEER

LEMON HAZELNUT SQUARES

## Salade Niçoise Sandwiches

*Make these ahead; they get better the longer they stand. Get things started with Mediterranean olives and cornichons, tiny brine-packed French pickles.*

**6 servings**

1    12½-OUNCE CAN TUNA PACKED IN WATER, WELL DRAINED

1    6⅛-OUNCE CAN TUNA PACKED IN WATER, WELL DRAINED

3    TABLESPOONS DRAINED CAPERS

¼    CUP MAYONNAISE

1½   TABLESPOONS FRESH LEMON JUICE

2    1-POUND SOFT FRENCH OR ITALIAN BREAD LOAVES

6    TABLESPOONS (ABOUT) OLIVE PASTE (OLIVADA) OR OLIVE SPREAD*

2    ½-OUNCE PACKAGES FRESH ARUGULA OR WATERCRESS

2    TOMATOES, SLICED

1    RED ONION, THINLY SLICED

Combine all tuna, capers, mayonnaise and fresh lemon juice in medium bowl. Season with pepper. Cut each bread loaf crosswise into 3 pieces, then halve each piece lengthwise. Pull out centers of bread pieces, leaving ½-inch-thick crusts. Spread olive paste on inside of each bread piece. Cover olive paste with generous amount of arugula. Spread ½ cup tuna mixture onto each bottom piece of bread. Top with sliced tomato and sliced onion, then with top pieces of bread. Wrap each sandwich tightly in foil. *(Can be prepared 6 hours ahead. Refrigerate.)*

*\*Available at Italian markets and specialty foods stores. If unavailable, puree ½ cup pitted, black, brine-cured olives (such as Kalamata) in processor or blender.*

## Green Bean Salad with Basil Vinaigrette

**6 servings**

2    POUNDS GREEN BEANS, TRIMMED

3    SHALLOTS, MINCED

2    TABLESPOONS BALSAMIC VINEGAR OR RED WINE VINEGAR

¼    CUP OLIVE OIL

⅔    CUP CHOPPED FRESH BASIL LEAVES

⅔    CUP GRATED ROMANO CHEESE

    ADDITIONAL GRATED ROMANO CHEESE

Cook beans in large pot of rapidly boiling salted water until just crisp-tender. Rinse with cold water. Drain. Transfer to bowl. Combine shallots and vinegar. Gradually mix in oil. Add basil. Add enough dressing to beans to coat. Gently mix in ⅔ cup cheese. Season with salt and pepper. *(Can be made 4 hours ahead. Cover; chill.)* Place beans on platter. Top with additional cheese.

## Lemon Hazelnut Squares

makes 16

**CRUST**

1    CUP ALL PURPOSE FLOUR

¼    CUP SUGAR

¼    TEASPOON SALT

6    TABLESPOONS (¾ STICK) CHILLED UNSALTED BUTTER, CUT INTO PIECES

¼    CUP CHOPPED HUSKED TOASTED HAZELNUTS

**FILLING**

¾    CUP SUGAR

2    EGGS

3    TABLESPOONS FRESH LEMON JUICE

1    TABLESPOON MINCED LEMON PEEL

½    TEASPOON BAKING POWDER

    POWDERED SUGAR

FOR CRUST: Preheat oven to 350°F. Line 8-inch square baking pan with foil; butter foil. Mix flour, sugar and salt in processor. Add butter and nuts and blend until fine meal forms. Press onto bottom of prepared pan. Bake until light brown around edges, about 18 minutes.

MEANWHILE, PREPARE FILLING: Blend first 6 ingredients in processor. Pour filling onto hot crust. Bake until filling begins to brown at edges and is just springy to touch, about 20 minutes. Cool completely in pan on rack. Lift foil and dessert from pan. Gently peel foil from edges. Cut dessert into 16 squares. *(Can be made 1 day ahead. Wrap tightly; chill.)* Sift powdered sugar over squares; serve at room temperature.

OPPOSITE: SALADE NIÇOISE SANDWICHES AND GREEN BEAN SALAD WITH BASIL VINAIGRETTE.

## MEMORIAL DAY BACK-YARD PICNIC *for* EIGHT

MIXED NUTS

ROASTED CHICKEN, BELL PEPPER *and* ONION SALAD

FRENCH BREAD *with* GOAT CHEESE *and* SUN-DRIED TOMATO SPREAD

CELERY STICKS *and* RADISHES

CHILLED BEAUJOLAIS

DOUBLE CHOCOLATE-CHERRY BROWNIES

## Roasted Chicken, Bell Pepper and Onion Salad

*Set bowls of mixed nuts around the back yard, and serve the salad with glasses of chilled Beaujolais wine.*

**8 servings**

CHICKEN AND VEGETABLES

- ⅔ CUP OLIVE OIL
- ⅔ CUP BALSAMIC VINEGAR OR RED WINE VINEGAR
- ¼ CUP CHOPPED FRESH ROSEMARY OR 2 TEASPOONS DRIED
- 5 GARLIC CLOVES, MINCED
- ½ TEASPOON DRIED CRUSHED RED PEPPER
- 4 POUNDS CHICKEN BREAST HALVES
- 3 LARGE RED BELL PEPPERS, CUT INTO ½-INCH-WIDE STRIPS
- 2 LARGE YELLOW BELL PEPPERS, CUT INTO ½-INCH-WIDE STRIPS
- 3 LARGE RED ONIONS, CUT INTO ½-INCH-THICK RINGS

DRESSING

- 2 TEASPOONS DIJON MUSTARD
- 2 TEASPOONS BALSAMIC VINEGAR OR RED WINE VINEGAR
- ¼ CUP OLIVE OIL
- 4 TEASPOONS GRATED ORANGE PEEL
- 1 TEASPOON CHOPPED FRESH ROSEMARY OR ½ TEASPOON DRIED

ORNAMENTAL KALE LEAVES
FRESH ROSEMARY SPRIGS

**FOR CHICKEN AND VEGETABLES:** Preheat oven to 425°F. Combine first 5 ingredients in medium bowl. Place chicken breasts in large baking pan. Divide vegetables among 2 large baking pans. Brush chicken on both sides with oil mixture. Sprinkle both sides with salt and pepper. Arrange skin side up in pan. Divide remaining oil mixture between pans of vegetables; mix to coat vegetables. Sprinkle with salt and pepper. Bake chicken until just cooked through, about 35 minutes, and vegetables until edges brown, about 40 minutes. Cool slightly.

**FOR DRESSING:** Combine mustard and vinegar in medium bowl. Gradually mix in oil. Add grated orange peel and chopped rosemary.

Remove skin and bones from chicken. Cut chicken into ½-inch-wide strips. Add to dressing and mix to coat. Season to taste with salt and pepper. Mix with roasted vegetables in large bowl. Season entire salad to taste with salt and pepper. *(Can be prepared 1 day ahead. Cover and refrigerate.)*

Line platter with kale. Spoon salad over. Garnish with rosemary sprigs.

## French Bread with Goat Cheese and Sun-dried Tomato Spread

*A perfect partner to the salad. Accompany with a platter of celery sticks and radishes with their tops attached.*

**8 servings**

- 1 11-OUNCE PACKAGE SOFT FRESH GOAT CHEESE (SUCH AS MONTRACHET)
- ⅔ CUP CHOPPED WALNUTS
- ½ CUP CHOPPED DRAINED OIL-PACKED SUN-DRIED TOMATOES
- 4 TEASPOONS MINCED FRESH THYME OR 1 TEASPOON DRIED
- ¼ CUP (ABOUT) SOUR CREAM

MINCED FRESH THYME
CHOPPED WALNUTS

- 2 FRENCH BREAD BAGUETTES, SLICED

Mix first 4 ingredients in bowl. Thin to spreadable consistency with sour cream. Season with generous amount of pepper. Mound cheese in crock or bowl. *(Can be prepared 2 days ahead. Cover and chill. Bring to room temperature before serving.)*

Sprinkle cheese with thyme and walnuts. Serve with bread.

## Double Chocolate-Cherry Brownies

*Dried sour cherries and a hint of cinnamon add an original twist to a tried-and-true standby. And you don't even need a mixing bowl: The batter is made in the saucepan with the melted chocolate.*

**makes 16 or 32**

- ¾ CUP (1½ STICKS) UNSALTED BUTTER
- 6 OUNCES UNSWEETENED CHOCOLATE, CHOPPED
- 2½ CUPS SUGAR
- 4 EGGS
- 1 EGG YOLK
- 1½ TEASPOONS VANILLA EXTRACT
- ½ TEASPOON ALMOND EXTRACT
- 1 CUP PLUS 2 TABLESPOONS ALL PURPOSE FLOUR
- 1 TEASPOON GROUND CINNAMON
- 1 CUP HALVED DRIED SOUR OR BING CHERRIES OR CHOPPED PITTED PRUNES
- 1 CUP SEMISWEET CHOCOLATE CHIPS

Preheat oven to 350°F. Butter and flour 13 x 8½-inch glass baking dish. Melt butter and unsweetened chocolate in heavy large saucepan over low heat, stirring until smooth. Remove from heat. Mix in sugar. Mix in eggs 1 at a time, then yolk. Add extracts, then flour and cinnamon and stir just until blended. Mix in cherries and chocolate chips.

Spread batter in prepared pan. Bake until brownies are firm around edges and tester inserted into center comes out with a few crumbs, about 35 minutes. Cool on rack. Cut into 16 or 32 pieces. *(Can be prepared 2 days ahead. Wrap brownies individually and store airtight at room temperature.)*

OPPOSITE: ROASTED CHICKEN, BELL PEPPER AND ONION SALAD.

# FATHER'S DAY

DAD'S DAY DOESN'T HAVE QUITE THE SAME "WEIGHT" THAT MOM'S DOES. SHE GOT HER HOLIDAY IN 1915; HE HAD TO WAIT FOR HIS UNTIL 1972. SHE GETS TREATED TO CHAMPAGNE, FLOWERS AND AN ELEGANT BRUNCH; HE GETS A BAD TIE, SUSPICIOUS COLOGNE AND USUALLY HAS TO GRILL HIS OWN MEAL IN THE BACK YARD. WE WOULD BE MORE INCLINED TO CHANGE THIS TRADITION IF DAD WEREN'T SO HAPPILY GOOD-NATURED ABOUT IT. HE WEARS THE TIE AND SPLASHES ON THE COLOGNE. AND THE ONE TIME IT WAS SUGGESTED DAD FORGO THE BARBECUE IN FAVOR OF BRUNCH, HE GOT QUITE TESTY.

AS FOR ACTUALLY TAKING OVER THE COOKING DUTIES AND LETTING THE OLD MAN RELAX ON A CHAISE, DON'T EVEN CONSIDER IT. AFTER ALL, HE WHO OWNS THE "I'M THE COOK, DAMN IT" APRON, OWNS THE GRILL. INSTEAD, STEER HIM TOWARD A BARBECUE CLASSIC, LIKE THE PULLED PORK SANDWICHES HERE, OR A NOT-TOO-STRENUOUS MENU, FEATURING FOODS THAT DAD LIKES TO COOK AND LOVES TO EAT. RED MEAT AND POTATOES ARE THE STARS, PLUS THERE ARE PLENTY OF VEGETABLES (DAD'S A MODERN, HEALTHY GUY) AND A KNOCKOUT FRESH FRUIT PIE À LA MODE FOR DESSERT. NOW, IF HE WOULD JUST TAKE OFF THAT APRON.

OPPOSITE: BUTTERFLIED LEG OF LAMB WITH ROSEMARY; RED POTATOES WITH OLIVES, FETA AND MINT; GRILLED BREAD WITH OLIVE OIL; AND GRILLED EGGPLANT, RED BELL PEPPER AND ARUGULA ROLLS.

## Butterflied Leg of Lamb with Rosemary

*The lamb needs to marinate for at least eight hours, so start the recipe ahead of time. This menu is nice with a light red wine, like Beaujolais.*

**6 servings**

- ¾ CUP DRY RED WINE
- ½ CUP EXTRA-VIRGIN OLIVE OIL
- ⅓ CUP COARSE-GRAINED MUSTARD
- ¼ CUP RED WINE VINEGAR
- 4 TABLESPOONS FRESH ROSEMARY LEAVES (6 SPRIGS)
- 2 TABLESPOONS DRAINED GREEN PEPPERCORNS IN BRINE
- 1 TABLESPOON DRIED OREGANO
- 2 LARGE GARLIC CLOVES

- 1 4- TO 5-POUND LEG OF LAMB, BONED, BUTTERFLIED, TRIMMED OF EXCESS FAT

Combine first 8 ingredients in blender. Puree until rosemary is completely ground, about 3 minutes.

Place lamb in large glass baking dish with 2-inch-high sides. Pour marinade over lamb, making certain all parts of lamb are covered with marinade. Cover; chill at least 8 hours or overnight. Let stand 2 hours at room temperature before cooking.

Prepare barbecue (medium-high heat). Remove lamb from marinade. Sprinkle both sides of lamb generously with salt and pepper. Grill lamb until brown and crusty on outside and thermometer inserted into thickest part registers 130°F for medium-rare, turning occasionally, about 20 minutes. Transfer to platter and tent with foil. Let stand 10 minutes. Cut on diagonal into thin slices and serve.

## Grilled Eggplant, Red Bell Pepper and Arugula Rolls

**6 servings**

- ¼ CUP BALSAMIC VINEGAR
- ¼ CUP OLIVE OIL
- 2 SMALL EGGPLANTS (1 POUND EACH), CUT LENGTHWISE INTO ¼-INCH-THICK SLICES

- 4 RED BELL PEPPERS

- 2 BUNCHES ARUGULA
- ½ CUP (ABOUT) PINE NUTS, TOASTED

Prepare barbecue (medium heat). Whisk together vinegar and oil. Season with salt and pepper. Brush both sides of eggplant slices with ¼ cup vinaigrette. Grill until cooked through, turning occasionally, about 4 minutes per side. Remove from grill; brush with ¼ cup vinaigrette. Cool.

Grill bell peppers until blackened on all sides. Wrap in paper bag and let stand 10 minutes. Peel and seed peppers. Cut into ¼-inch strips. Season peppers with salt and pepper. *(Can be made 1 day ahead. Cover; refrigerate eggplant and bell peppers separately.)*

Place eggplant slices on work surface. Place 4 bell pepper strips on 1 end of each eggplant slice; top with 2 to 4 arugula sprigs, allowing peppers and arugula to extend beyond both sides of eggplant. Sprinkle pine nuts atop arugula. Roll eggplant up. Place seam side down on platter. *(Can be prepared 4 hours ahead. Cover eggplant with plastic and store at room temperature.)*

## Red Potatoes with Olives, Feta and Mint

*This warm potato salad has a Mediterranean accent, thanks to mint, feta cheese and Kalamata olives.*

**6 servings**

1¾ POUNDS SMALL RED-SKINNED POTATOES, CUT INTO QUARTERS

1 BUNCH FRESH MINT, CHOPPED

8 OUNCES FETA CHEESE, CRUMBLED

¾ CUP BRINE-CURED BLACK OLIVES (SUCH AS KALAMATA), PITTED, CHOPPED

¼ CUP EXTRA-VIRGIN OLIVE OIL

Place potatoes and 3 tablespoons mint in large pot of salted water. Bring water to boil, reduce heat and simmer potatoes until tender, about 12 minutes. Drain; transfer to large bowl.

Set aside 2 tablespoons each of mint, cheese and olives; add remainder to warm potatoes. Mix in oil. Season with salt and pepper. Garnish with reserved mint, cheese and olives. Serve warm.

## Grilled Bread with Olive Oil

*In this recipe—for a change of pace from plain olive oil—try any of the oils currently on the market that are flavored with garlic, basil or rosemary.*

**6 servings**

1 FRENCH BREAD BAGUETTE, CUT INTO 1-INCH DIAGONAL SLICES

¼ CUP EXTRA-VIRGIN OLIVE OIL

Prepare barbecue (medium-high heat). Brush both sides of bread generously with oil; season with salt and pepper. Grill until golden, about 1 minute per side. Serve immediately.

## Fresh Peach Pie

*Serve this seasonal treat (below right) with vanilla ice cream.*

**6 to 8 servings**

**CRUST**

2¼ CUPS ALL PURPOSE FLOUR

1 TABLESPOON SUGAR

½ TEASPOON SALT

¾ CUP (1½ STICKS) CHILLED UNSALTED BUTTER, CUT INTO PIECES

1 TABLESPOON FRESH LEMON JUICE

6 TABLESPOONS (ABOUT) ICE WATER

**FILLING**

4¼ POUNDS RIPE PEACHES, PEELED, PITTED, CUT INTO ½-INCH-THICK WEDGES

¾ CUP FIRMLY PACKED GOLDEN BROWN SUGAR

¼ CUP ALL PURPOSE FLOUR

1 TABLESPOON GRATED LEMON PEEL

1¼ TEASPOONS GROUND CINNAMON

FOR CRUST: Mix flour, sugar and salt in processor. Cut in butter, using on/off turns, until mixture resembles coarse meal. Blend in lemon juice. Blend in enough water by tablespoonfuls until dough forms moist clumps. Gather dough into 2 balls; flatten each into disk. Wrap each in plastic and refrigerate 1 hour. *(Can be made 3 days ahead. Keep chilled. Let dough soften slightly at room temperature before rolling.)*

FOR FILLING: Preheat oven to 400°F. Mix all ingredients in large bowl. Let stand 5 minutes.

Roll out 1 dough disk on lightly floured surface to 13-inch round. Transfer to 9-inch-diameter deep-dish glass pie dish. Spoon filling into crust. Roll out second disk on lightly floured surface to 13-inch round. Arrange atop pie. Press edges together. Trim overhang to 1 inch. Fold overhang under. Crimp edges decoratively. Cut vents in top crust to allow steam to escape. Place pie on large baking sheet.

Bake pie 45 minutes. Reduce oven temperature to 350°F. Continue baking until juices bubble thickly, covering edges of crust with foil if becoming brown, about 15 minutes. Transfer pie to rack and cool completely.

## Pork Barbecue Sandwiches with Coleslaw

*The instructions given here are for a standard 22-inch Weber kettle barbecue. Grilling times and vent adjustments will vary with different types of barbecues.*

**makes 12 sandwiches**

### Barbecue Sauce

| | |
|---|---|
| ¼ | CUP (½ STICK) UNSALTED BUTTER |
| 6 | TABLESPOONS MINCED ONION |
| 1⅓ | CUPS CIDER VINEGAR |
| 1⅓ | CUPS KETCHUP |
| 1 | CUP FIRMLY PACKED DARK BROWN SUGAR |
| 1 | TEASPOON WORCESTERSHIRE SAUCE |
| ¼ | TEASPOON CAYENNE PEPPER |

### Dry Seasoning Rub

| | |
|---|---|
| 3 | TABLESPOONS COARSELY GROUND PEPPER |
| 3 | TABLESPOONS DARK BROWN SUGAR |
| 3 | TABLESPOONS PAPRIKA |
| 2 | TABLESPOONS SALT |
| 1 | TEASPOON CAYENNE PEPPER |

### Coleslaw

| | |
|---|---|
| 1 | CUP MAYONNAISE |
| 6 | TABLESPOONS CIDER VINEGAR |
| 6 | TABLESPOONS BARBECUE SAUCE (SEE RECIPE ABOVE) |
| 3 | TABLESPOONS SUGAR |
| 12 | CUPS LIGHTLY PACKED SHREDDED GREEN CABBAGE (ABOUT 2 SMALL HEADS) |

### Barbecue Mop

| | |
|---|---|
| 1 | CUP CIDER VINEGAR |
| ½ | CUP WATER |
| 1 | TABLESPOON WORCESTERSHIRE SAUCE |
| 1 | TABLESPOON COARSELY GROUND PEPPER |
| 1 | TABLESPOON SALT |
| 2 | TEASPOONS VEGETABLE OIL |
| ½ | TEASPOON CAYENNE PEPPER |

### Pork

| | |
|---|---|
| 2 | UNTRIMMED BONELESS PORK SHOULDER HALVES (ALSO KNOWN AS BOSTON BUTT; ABOUT 6 POUNDS TOTAL) |
| 4 | CUPS HICKORY WOOD (SMOKE) CHIPS |
| 1 | 20-POUND SACK CHARCOAL BRIQUETTES |
| 12 | SOFT HAMBURGER BUNS WITH SESAME SEEDS, WARM |

**FOR BARBECUE SAUCE:** Melt butter in heavy large saucepan over medium heat. Add onion and sauté 3 minutes. Add remaining ingredients and bring to boil, stirring frequently. Reduce heat and simmer until sauce is reduced to 2⅔ cups, stirring occasionally, about 30 minutes. Season to taste with salt and pepper. *(Sauce can be prepared 1 week ahead. Cover and refrigerate.)*

**FOR DRY SEASONING RUB:** Mix all ingredients in small bowl. *(Can be made 1 week ahead. Store airtight.)*

**FOR COLESLAW:** Mix first 4 ingredients in large bowl. Mix in cabbage. Season with salt and pepper. Refrigerate at least 1 hour. *(Can be prepared up to 1 day ahead. Keep refrigerated.)*

**I**F DAD HAD A THRONE, IT WOULD BE RIGHT OVER THERE NEXT TO THE BARBECUE, THE ROOST HE LIKES TO RULE. AND IF HE'S ANY KIND OF BARBECUE PURIST, HE'LL LIKE THIS RECIPE FOR HONEST-TO-GOODNESS PULLED PORK SANDWICHES: SLOW-COOKED PORK, KEPT MOIST WITH A VINEGARY MOP AND PILED ON A SOFT BUN WITH A GENEROUS AMOUNT OF RICH SAUCE AND FLAVORFUL COLE-SLAW. IT COMES FROM THE WESTERN EDGE OF NORTH CAROLINA, WHERE COOKING OVER A SMOKY FIRE HAS BEEN ELEVATED TO ART-FORM STATUS.

FOR BARBECUE MOP: Mix all ingredients in bowl. Set aside until ready to use.

FOR PORK: Place pork, fat side up, on work surface. Cut each pork piece lengthwise in half, forming total of 4 long strips. Place pork on baking sheet. Sprinkle Dry Seasoning Rub all over pork; rub into pork, covering completely. Cover and chill at least 2 hours and up to 6 hours.

Place wood chips in large bowl. Cover with cold water and let stand 30 minutes. Place handful of torn newspapers into bottom of charcoal chimney.* Top with 25 charcoal briquettes. Remove upper rack from barbecue grill. Place chimney on lower grill rack. Light newspaper and let charcoal burn until gray ash color, about 30 minutes.

Open 1 bottom grill vent. Turn out hot charcoal onto 1 side of lower rack. Using metal spatula, spread charcoal to cover approximately ⅓ of rack. Remove 1 cup of wood chips from water and drain (keep remaining chips in water). Scatter over coals (avoid using too many wet chips, which may douse the fire). Fill foil loaf pan halfway with water and place on lower grill rack on opposite side of coals.

Place upper grill rack on barbecue. Arrange pork, fat side up, on upper grill rack above loaf pan. Cover grill with lid, positioning top vent directly over pork. Place stem of candy thermometer through top vent, with gauge on outside and tip near pork (thermometer should not touch meat or grill rack); leave in place during cooking. Check temperature after 5 minutes. Use top and bottom vents to maintain temperature between 225° and 250°F, opening wider to increase heat and closing to decrease heat. Leave other vents closed.

After 30 minutes, use technique described above to light an additional 15 charcoal briquettes in same charcoal chimney set atop bricks, cement or other nonflammable surface.

When cooking temperature of barbecue falls below 225°F, use oven mitts to lift off upper grill rack with pork and place on heatproof surface. Using tongs, add half of hot gray charcoal to bottom rack. Sprinkle about 1 cup drained wood chips over charcoal. Reposition upper rack on barbecue with pork above loaf pan. Brush pork with Barbecue Mop. Cover with lid.

About once an hour, light more charcoal in chimney and replenish charcoal and wood chips as necessary to maintain temperature between 225°F and 250°F, brushing pork lightly with Barbecue Mop each time grill is opened. Open grill only when necessary and cover as quickly as possible to minimize loss of heat and smoke. Cook pork until meat thermometer inserted into center of meat registers between 165°F and 170°F, turning occasionally, about 3 hours total.

Transfer pork to baking sheet. Let stand 10 minutes. When cool enough to handle, shred pork into bite-size pieces, discarding any fat. Mix any meat juices accumulated on baking sheet into pork. Spoon pork onto bottom halves of buns. Drizzle with Barbecue Sauce. Top with Coleslaw and bun tops.

*Available at many cookware stores and some hardware stores.

1 USEFUL EQUIPMENT FOR MAKING THIS SLOW-COOKED PORK INCLUDES A THERMOMETER, A CHARCOAL CHIMNEY (HERE FILLED WITH CHARCOAL BRIQUETTES), WOOD CHIPS, A LONG SPATULA, FORK, TONGS, BRUSHES AND OVEN MITTS.

2 AFTER SPREADING HOT CHARCOAL TO COVER ONE-THIRD OF THE BOTTOM GRILL RACK, DRAIN ONE CUP OF SOAKED HICKORY WOOD CHIPS AND SCATTER THEM OVER THE COALS.

3 PLACE STEM OF CANDY THERMOMETER THROUGH TOP VENT (THERMOMETER SHOULD NOT TOUCH PORK OR GRILL RACK) TO CHECK THAT TEMPERATURE INSIDE BARBECUE IS MAINTAINED AT 225°F TO 250°F.

4 EACH TIME THE GRILL IS OPENED, USE A BRUSH TO APPLY A LIGHT COATING OF BARBECUE MOP OVER PORK; KEEP GRILL CLOSED AS MUCH AS POSSIBLE.

# THE FOURTH OF JULY

This is the holiday of sizzle and smoke. Fireworks sparkle in the sky while grills glow in yards across the land. In celebration of the signing of this great democracy's Declaration of Independence, the ultimate assertion of its individuality, we all gather around smoldering fires—and cook the same darned thing we always do. When it comes to the Fourth of July menu, some revolutionary spirit seems to have been lost. Firm believers that a touch or two of tradition is essential to the proper appreciation of family events, we also think the spirit of this particular holiday calls for more than a little culinary rebellion, tempered with a comfortable touch of the familiar.

To that end, there are a number of recipes here that take tradition and tweak it a little, including some terrific barbecue sauces, and a version of fried chicken with real bite. In our grill menu, the true but tired cheeseburger gets replaced by turkey burgers stuffed with goat cheese and the expected corn on the cob takes a backseat to a basil-scented corn and tomato gratin. Dessert (it would be un-American not to serve one) is creamy cheesecake with a caramel and banana topping.

Opposite: Goat Cheese-stuffed Turkey Burgers with Roasted Red Pepper Relish; Corn and Tomato Gratin with Basil; and Bananas Foster Cheesecake.

## FOURTH OF JULY DINNER *for* SIX

GOAT CHEESE-STUFFED
TURKEY BURGERS *with*
ROASTED RED PEPPER RELISH

ASSORTED PICKLES *and* OLIVES

CORN *and* TOMATO GRATIN
*with* BASIL

CHARDONNAY

BANANAS FOSTER CHEESECAKE

## Goat Cheese-stuffed Turkey Burgers with Roasted Red Pepper Relish

*The goat cheese and relish keep these burgers especially moist. For a nice variation, omit the goat cheese, and top the turkey burgers with sliced Havarti or Monterey Jack cheese during the last few minutes of cooking. Set out bowls of pickles and olives, and pour chilled Chardonnay throughout the meal.*

**6 servings**

| | |
|---|---|
| 1½ | POUNDS LEAN GROUND TURKEY |
| 6 | TABLESPOONS FRESH BREADCRUMBS |
| 3 | TABLESPOONS FRESH LEMON JUICE |
| 2 | TEASPOONS GRATED LEMON PEEL |
| 2 | TEASPOONS DRIED THYME |
| 1⅛ | TEASPOONS SALT |
| ½ | TEASPOON PEPPER |
| 6 | TABLESPOONS SOFT FRESH GOAT CHEESE (SUCH AS MONTRACHET) |
| 6 | WHOLE WHEAT HAMBURGER BUNS |
| | ROASTED RED PEPPER RELISH (SEE RECIPE AT RIGHT) |

Combine turkey, breadcrumbs, lemon juice, lemon peel, thyme, salt and pepper in large bowl. Mix well. Divide turkey mixture into 6 equal portions. Form 1 portion into two 4-inch-diameter patties. Place 1 tablespoon goat cheese atop 1 turkey patty; place second patty atop cheese. Seal patties at edges to enclose cheese. Repeat with remaining 5 portions. *(Can be prepared 4 hours ahead. Cover and refrigerate.)*

Prepare barbecue (medium-high heat). Grill burgers until cooked through, about 5 minutes per side. Grill hamburger buns, cut side down, until lightly toasted, about 1 minute. Place turkey burgers on bottom half of buns. Top burgers with Roasted Red Pepper Relish, then bun tops and serve.

## Roasted Red Pepper Relish

*Purchased roasted sweet red peppers, available in jars, make this snappy relish especially easy to prepare.*

**makes about 2 cups**

| | |
|---|---|
| 3 | TABLESPOONS OLIVE OIL |
| 4 | 7-OUNCE JARS ROASTED SWEET RED PEPPERS, RINSED, DRAINED, PATTED DRY, CHOPPED |
| 1½ | CUPS CHOPPED ONIONS |
| 3 | TEASPOONS FINELY CHOPPED GARLIC |
| 4½ | TABLESPOONS CIDER VINEGAR |
| 3 | TABLESPOONS SUGAR |
| ¼ | TEASPOON DRY MUSTARD |
| ¼ | TEASPOON CAYENNE PEPPER |

Heat oil in heavy large skillet over medium-high heat. Add red peppers and sauté 2 minutes. Add onions and garlic. Cook until onions are tender, stirring frequently, about 5 minutes.

Mix vinegar and sugar in small bowl until sugar dissolves. Stir vinegar mixture into red peppers. Mix in mustard and cayenne pepper. Season with salt. Continue cooking relish until all liquid has evaporated, stirring frequently, about 6 minutes. Cool to room temperature. *(Can be prepared 1 day ahead. Cover and refrigerate. Bring to room temperature before using.)*

## Corn and Tomato Gratin with Basil

*Fresh corn gets dressed up in this creamy, tasty side dish.*

**6 servings**

2   TABLESPOONS OLIVE OIL
1½   CUPS CHOPPED ONIONS
5   CUPS FRESH CORN KERNELS (FROM ABOUT 7 EARS)
⅛   TEASPOON GROUND NUTMEG

NONSTICK VEGETABLE OIL SPRAY

2½   CUPS HALF AND HALF
3   LARGE EGGS
2   LARGE EGG WHITES
¼   TEASPOON HOT PEPPER SAUCE

2   CUPS DICED SEEDED TOMATOES, DRAINED
½   CUP CHOPPED FRESH BASIL

Preheat oven to 350°F. Heat olive oil in heavy large skillet over medium-high heat. Add chopped onions to skillet. Sauté until onions are translucent, about 4 minutes. Add corn kernels and sauté until cooked through, about 6 minutes. Stir in ground nutmeg. Season with salt and pepper. Cool.

Spray 2-quart glass baking dish with nonstick vegetable oil spray. Combine half and half, eggs, egg whites and hot pepper sauce in large bowl and whisk to blend. Stir corn mixture into custard. Pour into prepared dish. Bake until custard is set, about 30 minutes.

Remove gratin from oven. Season tomatoes with salt and pepper. Sprinkle evenly over gratin. Bake until tomatoes are heated through, about 8 minutes. Sprinkle with basil and serve.

## Bananas Foster Cheesecake

*This cool indulgence is actually made with light cream cheese and low-fat sour cream. Begin preparing it a day ahead.*

**10 servings**

CRUST

¾   CUP ALL PURPOSE FLOUR
¾   CUP FINELY CHOPPED PECANS
4   TABLESPOONS (½ STICK) UNSALTED BUTTER, MELTED
3   TABLESPOONS SUGAR
2   TABLESPOONS FIRMLY PACKED GOLDEN BROWN SUGAR
1½   TEASPOONS VANILLA EXTRACT

FILLING

2   8-OUNCE PACKAGES NEUFCHÂTEL CHEESE (REDUCED-FAT CREAM CHEESE), ROOM TEMPERATURE
1¼   CUPS SUGAR
2   TABLESPOONS CORNSTARCH
3   LARGE EGGS
2   CUPS PUREED BANANAS (FROM ABOUT 4 BANANAS)
1   CUP LOW-FAT SOUR CREAM
1½   TABLESPOONS FRESH LEMON JUICE
1   TEASPOON VANILLA EXTRACT
1   TEASPOON GROUND CINNAMON
    PINCH OF SALT

TOPPING

1   CUP LOW-FAT SOUR CREAM
¼   CUP SUGAR
¼   TEASPOON VANILLA EXTRACT

1   17-OUNCE JAR CARAMEL SAUCE
2   TABLESPOONS DARK RUM
2   BANANAS, PEELED, SLICED

FOR CRUST: Position rack in center of oven and preheat to 350°F. Wrap outside of 9-inch-diameter springform pan with 3-inch-high sides with heavy-duty foil. Combine flour, pecans, butter, sugar, brown sugar and vanilla in large bowl. Mix well. Press mixture onto bottom of prepared pan.

FOR FILLING: Using electric mixer, beat cream cheese in large bowl until smooth. Gradually beat in sugar. Beat in cornstarch. Add eggs, 1 at a time, beating until just blended after each addition. Add pureed bananas, sour cream, lemon juice, vanilla, cinnamon and salt. Beat just until combined.

Transfer filling to crust-lined pan. Place pan in large roasting pan. Add enough hot water to roasting pan to come 1 inch up sides of springform pan. Bake until center of cake is just set, about 1 hour 15 minutes. Remove cake from oven. Maintain oven temperature.

MEANWHILE, PREPARE TOPPING: Mix together sour cream, sugar and vanilla in small bowl until well blended.

Spread topping over cheesecake. Bake until topping is set, about 10 minutes. Turn off oven. Let cake stand in oven until cooled to room temperature, about 2 hours. Refrigerate until well chilled. Cover and chill overnight.

Cut around cake to loosen; remove pan sides. Transfer cake to platter. Warm caramel sauce in small saucepan over low heat, stirring often. Mix in rum. Drizzle some sauce decoratively over cake. Arrange bananas atop cake. Cut cake into wedges. Serve, passing remaining sauce separately.

# HOW *to* MAKE *the* BEST FRIED CHICKEN

## Spicy Fried Chicken

**4 servings**

### MARINATING CHICKEN

| | |
|---|---|
| 6 | MEDIUM GARLIC CLOVES |
| 2 | CUPS BUTTERMILK |
| 1¼ | TEASPOONS GROUND CUMIN |
| ½ | TEASPOON SALT |
| ½ | TEASPOON PEPPER |
| ¼ | TEASPOON CAYENNE PEPPER |
| 1 | 3½-POUND FRYER, CUT INTO 8 PIECES |

### COATING CHICKEN

| | |
|---|---|
| 1½ | CUPS UNBLEACHED ALL PURPOSE FLOUR |
| 1¾ | TEASPOONS SALT |
| 1½ | TEASPOONS PEPPER |
| ½ | TEASPOON GROUND CUMIN |
| ½ | TEASPOON CAYENNE PEPPER |

### FRYING

SAFFLOWER OIL
(FOR DEEP FRYING)

CHOPPED FRESH CILANTRO
LIME WEDGES

If your INDEPENDENCE DAY CELEBRATION TAKES YOU AWAY FROM THE GRILL—TO A BEACH, A PARK, MAYBE THE TOP OF A MOUNTAIN—THERE'S ALWAYS FRIED CHICKEN, THE BEST KIND OF PORTABLE FOOD. BUT HOW TO GET IT CRISP ON THE OUTSIDE, TENDER AND JUICY WITHIN, NICELY SPICED BUT NOT TOO HOT? THIS RECIPE SHOWS HOW, STEP BY STEP. ADD BISCUITS, COLESLAW AND BEER AND YOU HAVE A MEAL TO CELEBRATE.

**FOR MARINATING CHICKEN:** Mash garlic with flat side of knife. Place garlic in medium bowl. Add buttermilk, cumin, salt, pepper and cayenne and whisk to blend. Place chicken pieces in 13 x 9-inch glass baking dish. Pour buttermilk mixture over; turn chicken to coat. Cover and chill at least 8 hours or overnight, turning occasionally.

Place rack over baking sheet. Remove chicken from marinade and set on rack. Let drain 10 minutes.

FOR COATING CHICKEN: Mix flour, salt, pepper, cumin and cayenne pepper in large bowl. Toss chicken pieces in batches in flour mixture, turning to coat; shake off excess. Toss each piece again in flour mixture; shake off excess. Transfer chicken to rack on baking sheet. Let stand at least 15 minutes and up to 45 minutes.

FOR FRYING: Preheat oven to low. Line baking sheet with paper towels. Pour oil into heavy large skillet to depth of ¾ inch. Heat oil over high heat to 375°F or until small cube of fresh bread sizzles instantly when added. Add chicken thigh and leg pieces to skillet. Adjust heat so that temperature remains between 340°F and 350°F or until small cube of bread sizzles slowly when added. Fry until chicken is golden brown and cooked through, turning chicken occasionally, about 16 minutes. Using tongs, transfer chicken to paper towel-lined baking sheet. Place baking sheet with chicken in oven to keep warm.

Reheat oil to 375°F. Add breast and wing pieces to skillet. Adjust heat so that temperature remains between 340°F and 350°F and fry chicken until cooked through and golden brown, turning occasionally with tongs, about 10 minutes. Using tongs, transfer chicken to prepared sheet and drain.

Transfer chicken to platter. Sprinkle with cilantro. Garnish with lime wedges. Serve hot, warm or let stand up to 2 hours at room temperature.

**1** FLAT SIDE OF KNIFE IS USED TO MASH THE GARLIC. THE PAPERY GARLIC SKIN IS THEN DISCARDED.

**2** BUTTERMILK, GARLIC, CUMIN, CAYENNE, SALT AND PEPPER ARE MIXED AND POURED OVER THE CHICKEN PIECES. THE CHICKEN MUST MARINATE IN THE REFRIGERATOR AT LEAST EIGHT HOURS.

**3** AFTER BEING REMOVED FROM MARINADE AND DRAINED, THE CHICKEN PIECES ARE DREDGED TWICE IN SEASONED FLOUR. BEFORE FRYING, CHICKEN IS AIR-DRIED 15 TO 45 MINUTES.

**4** A PIECE OF BREAD IS ADDED TO THE HOT OIL AS A TEMPERATURE TEST. IF THE BREAD SIZZLES INSTANTLY, THE OIL IS HOT ENOUGH FOR DEEP FRYING.

**5** CHICKEN IS FRIED UNTIL DEEP BROWN AND COOKED THROUGH. EVEN COOKING IS ENSURED BY TURNING THE CHICKEN FREQUENTLY WITH TONGS.

# GREAT BARBECUE SAUCES

**F**OR MANY, THE FOURTH OF JULY SIGNALS THE START OF THE GRILLING SEASON, THOSE COUPLE OF SUMMER MONTHS WHEN IT'S JUST TOO HOT TO COOK IN THE KITCHEN. SO HOW TO ADD VARIETY TO THE FOODS YOU'LL BE GRILLING FOR THE NEXT 60 DAYS? WITH THESE SAUCES AND MARINADES.

THERE'S SOMETHING HERE FOR EVERYONE, FROM THE EXOTIC TO THE TRADITIONAL, ALL OF THEM EASY TO MAKE AND EASILY MADE AHEAD.

## Caribbean Coconut-Curry Sauce

*The recipe makes enough for 1 1/2 pounds of chicken or shrimp.*

**makes about 1½ cups**

- 2/3 CUP CANNED CREAM OF COCONUT (SUCH AS COCO LOPEZ)*
- ½ CUP FRESH LIME JUICE
- 6 TABLESPOONS MINCED GREEN ONIONS
- 2 TEASPOONS CURRY POWDER
- ½ TEASPOON CAYENNE PEPPER
- ½ TEASPOON SALT

Whisk cream of coconut and fresh lime juice in small bowl until smooth. Stir in green onions, curry powder, cayenne pepper and salt. *(Can be made 1 day ahead. Cover and refrigerate.)*

Brush half of sauce over chicken or seafood before and during grilling. Pass remaining sauce separately.

*\*Available in most supermarkets.*

## Boilermaker Sauce

*A boilermaker is a classic one-two drink consisting of a shot of whiskey followed by a beer chaser. Those ingredients also come together in this all-American barbecue sauce. Use it on ribs, pork chops, chicken, even burgers (brush it on during the last ten minutes of grilling). If making ribs, brush them often during the first part of cooking with a mixture of one part cider vinegar to ten parts water and a pinch of dried crushed red pepper; that will keep them moist. This recipe makes enough for three pounds of meat or poultry and can be doubled easily.*

**makes about 2 cups**

- 2 TABLESPOONS VEGETABLE OIL
- 1 MEDIUM ONION, FINELY CHOPPED
- 2 LARGE GARLIC CLOVES, MINCED
- 1 12-OUNCE BOTTLE CHILI SAUCE
- ¾ CUP BEER
- ¼ CUP UNSULFURED (LIGHT) MOLASSES
- 3 TABLESPOONS CIDER VINEGAR
- 3 TABLESPOONS BOURBON WHISKEY
- 1½ TEASPOONS WORCESTERSHIRE SAUCE
- ½ TEASPOON HOT PEPPER SAUCE (SUCH AS TABASCO)

Heat oil in heavy medium saucepan over medium heat. Add onion and garlic; sauté until tender, about 8 minutes. Reduce heat. Add chili sauce, beer, molasses, vinegar, bourbon and Worcestershire sauce. Simmer until reduced to 2 cups, stirring occasionally, about 25 minutes. Stir in hot pepper sauce. *(Can be made up to 1 month ahead. Cover; refrigerate.)*

## Hunt Country Marinade

*This marinade (opposite, in jar) adds rich flavor to beef, venison, duck and game hens. The recipe makes enough to marinate two to three pounds of meat or poultry. It is important to remember that any marinade coming in contact with raw meat, seafood or poultry must be boiled for one minute before using it for basting.*

**makes about 1½ cups**

- ¾ CUP CABERNET SAUVIGNON OR OTHER DRY RED WINE
- ¼ CUP BALSAMIC VINEGAR
- 3 TABLESPOONS OLIVE OIL
- 2 TABLESPOONS UNSULFURED (LIGHT) MOLASSES
- 2 TABLESPOONS CHOPPED FRESH THYME OR 2 TEASPOONS DRIED
- 2 TABLESPOONS CHOPPED FRESH ROSEMARY OR 2 TEASPOONS DRIED
- 1 TABLESPOON CRUSHED JUNIPER BERRIES OR 2 TABLESPOONS GIN
- 3 LARGE GARLIC CLOVES, MINCED
- 3 2 X 1-INCH STRIPS ORANGE PEEL (ORANGE PART ONLY)
- 3 2 X 1-INCH STRIPS LEMON PEEL (YELLOW PART ONLY)
- 8 WHOLE CLOVES
- 8 WHOLE BLACK PEPPERCORNS
- 2 BAY LEAVES, BROKEN IN HALF
- ¾ TEASPOON SALT

Mix all ingredients in medium bowl. *(Can be made 2 days ahead. Cover; chill.)*

Marinate poultry 2 to 4 hours and meat 6 to 12 hours in refrigerator. Drain marinade into saucepan. Boil 1 minute. Pat meat or poultry dry. Grill, basting occasionally with marinade.

## Triple-Mustard Sauce

*Mustard and honey are a combination that's ideal for lamb or tuna steaks. It's a bit too pungent to use for dipping, but the flavor mellows with cooking. Brush the sauce (below, in bowl) liberally on meat or fish before and during grilling. The recipe makes enough for about 1 ½ pounds of lamb or fish.*

**makes generous ¾ cup**

- ¼ CUP DIJON MUSTARD
- 1 TEASPOON DRY MUSTARD
- 1 TEASPOON WHOLE MUSTARD SEEDS
- 1 TEASPOON CRUSHED BLACK PEPPERCORNS
- 3 TABLESPOONS BRANDY
- 3 TABLESPOONS CHOPPED FRESH TARRAGON OR 2 TEASPOONS DRIED
- 2 TABLESPOONS OLIVE OIL
- 1½ TABLESPOONS TARRAGON WHITE WINE VINEGAR OR WHITE WINE VINEGAR
- 2 TEASPOONS HONEY

Stir first 4 ingredients in bowl until dry mustard dissolves. Mix in remaining ingredients. Let sauce stand for 15 minutes. *(Can be made 3 days ahead. Cover and refrigerate.)*

## Five-Spice Shanghai Marinade

*Fragrant five-spice powder enhances the Asian accent in this recipe. Use it to marinate beef or chicken, and brush with the marinade while grilling. It is also delicious with seafood, but only needs to be brushed on during grilling. The recipe makes enough to marinate one pound of meat, poultry or seafood, with some left over to pass alongside.*

**makes about 1 cup**

- ⅔ CUP MINCED GREEN ONIONS
- ¼ CUP SOY SAUCE
- ¼ CUP DRY SHERRY
- 2 TABLESPOONS MINCED PEELED FRESH GINGER
- 2 TABLESPOONS CHILI OIL*
- 2 TEASPOONS ORIENTAL SESAME OIL
- 2 TEASPOONS FIVE-SPICE POWDER

Whisk all ingredients in medium bowl until blended. *(Can be prepared 1 day ahead. Cover and refrigerate.)*

Marinate beef or chicken in half of five-spice marinade at least 1 hour and up to 3 hours in refrigerator before grilling. Remove beef or chicken from marinade; boil marinade 1 minute. Brush boiled marinade over beef or chicken while grilling and pass remaining half of marinade separately.

*\*Available at Asian markets and in the Asian section of some supermarkets*

91

# LABOR DAY

As Memorial Day has evolved into a two-part holiday with both a serious and a festive side, so too has Labor Day come to be more than a single celebration. Enacted to honor the country's working men and women, it is now also a last fling with summer, one final three-day weekend of good times and great food before the chores and obligations we've been avoiding for the last three months finally regain our attention. While weeks of fine weather may yet lie ahead, Labor Day seems to signal the end of summer and a return to our responsibilities.

And after a full season of burgers and hot dogs, it's nice to anticipate the more formal entertaining of autumn with a rather elegant, yet still simple, dinner for friends. Pâté starts things off on the right note, followed by a beautiful salmon dish that gets served with a clever rendition of pommes Anna and a watercress and pear salad. An apple tart and chocolate truffles conclude the meal in style. And if those friends are staying the weekend, you'll also find easy solutions for Saturday lunch and Sunday breakfast in the pages that follow.

Opposite: Laquered Salmon; Mixed Pommes Anna; and Watercress, Pear and Walnut Salad with Poppy Seed Dressing.

## Chicken Liver Pâté

*This is quick, easy and delicious—a nice beginning to an elegant meal.*

**makes about 4 cups**

1½  POUNDS CHICKEN LIVERS,
    TRIMMED

¾   CUP (1½ STICKS) BUTTER,
    ROOM TEMPERATURE

½   CUP MINCED ONION

2   TABLESPOONS BRANDY

7   CANNED ANCHOVY FILLETS,
    DRAINED

¼   TEASPOON GROUND ALLSPICE

¼   TEASPOON GROUND NUTMEG

⅛   TEASPOON CAYENNE PEPPER

LEMON SLICES

WATERCRESS

ASSORTED CRACKERS AND
BAGUETTE SLICES

Cook chicken livers in large pot of simmering salted water until tender and cooked through, about 10 minutes. Drain chicken livers; cool.

Melt ¼ cup butter in heavy large skillet over medium-high heat. Add onion and sauté until tender, about 5 minutes. Add brandy and bring to boil. Remove from heat. Cool completely.

Finely grind livers, onion mixture, anchovies and remaining ½ cup butter in processor. Add allspice, nutmeg and cayenne pepper. Transfer to serving bowl. Refrigerate at least 1 hour. *(Can be prepared 2 days ahead. Keep chilled.)*

Garnish pâté with lemon slices and watercress. Serve pâté with crackers and baguette slices.

## Lacquered Salmon

*The salmon fillets are glazed with an Asian-style sauce that gives the baked fish a shiny, lacquered look.*

**8 servings**

2   CUPS SOY SAUCE

2   TABLESPOONS CORNSTARCH

2   TABLESPOONS ORIENTAL
    SESAME OIL

2   TABLESPOONS MINCED PEELED
    FRESH GINGER

2   TABLESPOONS RICE WINE
    OR DRY SHERRY

1   TABLESPOON HONEY

1   TEASPOON HOT PEPPER SAUCE
    (SUCH AS TABASCO)

1   TEASPOON PEPPER

2   GARLIC CLOVES, CHOPPED

½   TEASPOON GROUND TURMERIC

8   8-OUNCE SALMON FILLETS
    (ABOUT 1 INCH THICK)

2   BUNCHES GREEN ONIONS,
    ENDS TRIMMED

⅔   CUP WATER (OPTIONAL)

CHOPPED GREEN ONIONS

Puree first 10 ingredients in blender until almost smooth. *(Can be prepared 1 day ahead. Cover and refrigerate.)*

Preheat oven to 400°F. Lightly oil 2 medium baking dishes. Divide fish between prepared dishes. Add 1 bunch whole green onions to each dish. Pour half of sauce over fish, dividing between dishes. Bake until fish is just cooked through, basting frequently with remaining sauce and adding ⅓ cup water to each dish if sauce begins to burn, about 20 minutes. Arrange fish and baked green onions on plates; garnish with chopped green onions.

## Mixed Pommes Anna

*This lovely side dish is a variation of the French classic,* pommes Anna.

8 servings

1 CUP (2 STICKS) BUTTER

2 POUNDS WHITE BOILING
   POTATOES, PEELED,
   VERY THINLY SLICED

1 POUND SWEET POTATOES,
   PEELED, VERY THINLY SLICED

1 POUND RED-SKINNED POTATOES,
   VERY THINLY SLICED

1 TABLESPOON CHOPPED
   FRESH OREGANO

1 TABLESPOON CHOPPED
   FRESH THYME

To clarify butter, melt in small saucepan. Remove from heat; let stand 5 minutes. Using spoon, skim froth and solids from surface. Carefully pour clear melted butter into glass measuring cup, discarding any milky sediment remaining in saucepan.

Preheat oven to 450°F. Drizzle 2 table-spoons clarified butter into bottom of 10-inch-diameter ovenproof skillet with 2-inch-high sides. Swirl skillet to coat bottom. Placing all potatoes between layers of kitchen towels, dry potatoes well. Arrange half of white potatoes in overlapping circular pattern in prepared skillet. Season with salt and pepper. Drizzle with 2 tablespoons clarified butter. Arrange half of sweet potatoes in overlapping circular pattern over white potatoes. Season with salt and pepper. Drizzle with 2 tablespoons clarified butter. Arrange half of red-skinned potatoes in overlapping circular pattern over sweet potatoes. Season with salt and pepper. Drizzle with 2 tablespoons clarified butter. Repeat layering with remaining potatoes, drizzling each layer with clarified butter. Press on potatoes to compact. Cover skillet with foil.

Bake potatoes 25 minutes. Uncover and bake until potatoes are tender and top is golden, about 1 hour 15 minutes. Run sharp knife around edge of potatoes. Turn out potato cake onto platter. Sprinkle with herbs; cut into wedges.

## Watercress, Pear and Walnut Salad with Poppy Seed Dressing

8 servings

3 TABLESPOONS APPLE CIDER
   VINEGAR

4 TEASPOONS DIJON MUSTARD

1 TABLESPOON HONEY

¾ CUP CORN OIL

1 TEASPOON POPPY SEEDS

2 LARGE BUNCHES WATERCRESS,
   TRIMMED

⅔ CUPS WALNUTS, TOASTED,
   CHOPPED

2 PEARS, PEELED, CUT INTO
   ¾-INCH PIECES

Whisk vinegar, mustard and honey in small bowl to blend. Gradually whisk in oil. Mix in poppy seeds. Season dressing to taste with salt and pepper.

Toss watercress and walnuts in large bowl with enough dressing to coat. Season with salt and pepper. Divide salad among 8 plates. Toss pears with ¼ cup dressing in small bowl. Spoon pears atop salads and serve.

## Golden Delicious Apple Tart

*Both the filling and the crust of this sophisticated tart (opposite) can be made ahead.*

8 servings

CRUST

1¼ CUPS ALL PURPOSE FLOUR

¼ CUP SUGAR

½ TEASPOON SALT

10 TABLESPOONS (1¼ STICKS)
    CHILLED UNSALTED BUTTER,
    CUT INTO PIECES

1 LARGE EGG YOLK

1 TABLESPOON COLD WATER

FILLING

2 LARGE EGG YOLKS

6 TABLESPOONS SUGAR

1 TABLESPOON CORNSTARCH

⅓ CUP WHIPPING CREAM

⅓ CUP FROZEN APPLE JUICE
   CONCENTRATE, THAWED

3 TABLESPOONS UNSALTED BUTTER

3 LARGE GOLDEN DELICIOUS
   APPLES, PEELED, CORED,
   EACH CUT INTO 16 SLICES

FOR CRUST: Mix flour, sugar and salt in medium bowl. Add butter and rub in until mixture resembles coarse meal. Whisk yolk and water in small bowl. Add to flour mixture and mix just until dough clumps together. Gather dough into ball; flatten into disk. Cover with plastic wrap and chill 1 hour.

Soften dough slightly at room temperature. Press dough evenly over bottom and up sides of 9-inch-diameter tart pan with removable bottom. Trim excess dough and reserve. Freeze crust until firm, about 25 minutes.

Preheat oven to 400°F. Line crust with foil; fill with dried beans or pie weights. Bake until sides are set, about 15 minutes. Remove foil and beans. Bake until light golden, piercing bottom with fork if crust bubbles and patching with reserved dough if crust cracks, 10 minutes longer. Cool on rack.

FOR FILLING: Whisk egg yolks, 2 tablespoons sugar and cornstarch in medium bowl to blend. Bring whipping cream and apple juice concentrate to simmer in heavy medium saucepan. Whisk into yolk mixture. Return mixture to same saucepan and whisk over medium heat until mixture boils and thickens, about 2 minutes. Transfer to bowl and cool. (*Can be prepared 1 day ahead. Store crust at room temperature; refrigerate filling.*)

Preheat oven to 375°F. Melt butter in heavy large skillet over medium heat. Add apples and sauté until tender and light golden, about 10 minutes. Add 3 tablespoons sugar; toss until sugar dissolves and apples are glazed, about 3 minutes. Cool 15 minutes.

Spread cream filling over bottom of crust. Arrange apples in concentric circles atop filling. Bake tart 15 minutes. Sprinkle with 1 tablespoon sugar; bake until filling is set and apples are glazed, about 10 minutes longer. Serve tart slightly warm or at room temperature.

I F YOU ARE CELEBRATING THE LAST WEEKEND OF SUMMER WITH FRIENDS, SOME OF WHOM WILL LIKELY BE HOUSEGUESTS, YOU MAY FIND YOURSELF WHIPPING UP LUNCH ON SATURDAY AND SOMETHING FOR A LATE BREAKFAST ON SUNDAY.

HERE ARE TWO RECIPES SURE TO MAKE WEEKEND ENTERTAINING EASY: A CHICKEN-NOODLE SOUP YOU CAN PREPARE AHEAD AND KEEP ON HAND (ADD CRUSTY BREAD AND A SALAD FOR A LIGHT LUNCH) AND A QUICK-TO-MAKE BAKED EGG DISH (ROUND OUT THE MEAL WITH SWEET ROLLS AND BAKED FRUIT FOR DESSERT).

## Chicken, Corn and Noodle Soup with Saffron

**8 servings**

- 9 CUPS CANNED LOW-SALT CHICKEN BROTH
- 1 3-POUND CUT-UP CHICKEN; NECK, GIZZARD AND HEART RESERVED

- 3 TABLESPOONS BUTTER
- 2 CUPS CHOPPED ONIONS
- 1 CUP DICED PEELED CARROTS
- ¾ CUP DICED CELERY
- 2 LARGE GARLIC CLOVES, MINCED
- ¼ TEASPOON DRIED THYME
- ¼ TEASPOON CRUMBLED SAFFRON THREADS
- 2 OUNCES DRIED WIDE EGG NOODLES
- 1 CUP FROZEN CORN KERNELS
- 2 TABLESPOONS MINCED FRESH PARSLEY
- 2 TABLESPOONS MINCED CELERY LEAVES

Combine broth, chicken pieces, neck, gizzard and heart in large pot. Bring to boil. Reduce heat; cover partially and simmer until chicken is cooked through, about 20 minutes. Using tongs, remove chicken pieces and giblets from broth. Cool slightly. Remove skin from breasts and leg-thigh pieces. Cut enough chicken meat to measure 1 cup. Reserve remaining cooked chicken for another use. Strain broth into large bowl. Chill broth until fat solidifies on surface, about 6 hours. *(Broth can be made 2 days ahead. Keep chilled.)* Scrape fat from surface of broth and discard.

Melt butter in heavy large pot over medium-low heat. Add onions, carrots, celery, garlic and thyme. Cover; cook until vegetables soften, stirring occasionally, about 10 minutes. Add broth and bring to boil. Reduce heat; simmer until vegetables are almost tender, about 15 minutes. Add saffron. *(Can be made 1 day ahead. Cover; chill. Bring to boil before continuing.)* Add noodles; simmer 5 minutes. Add 1 cup chicken and corn; simmer until noodles are tender, about 5 minutes. Add parsley and celery leaves. Season with salt and pepper and serve.

## Eggs Florentine Plus

*The traditional egg and spinach dish is embellished with smoked turkey and porcini mushrooms.*

**6 servings**

- 1 OUNCE DRIED PORCINI MUSHROOMS*
- 1 14½-OUNCE CAN LOW-SALT CHICKEN BROTH

- 3 TABLESPOONS BUTTER
- 1 10-OUNCE PACKAGE READY-CUT FRESH SPINACH, STEMS TRIMMED

- 1 CUP CHOPPED ONION
- 2 TABLESPOONS ALL PURPOSE FLOUR
- 2 TABLESPOONS WHIPPING CREAM
- 12 OUNCES SMOKED TURKEY BREAST, CUT INTO ½-INCH CUBES

- 6 EGGS
- ⅓ CUP GRATED PARMESAN CHEESE
  TOASTED COUNTRY-STYLE BREAD

Rinse porcini under running water; place in bowl. Bring broth to boil in medium saucepan. Pour over porcini. Let stand until soft, about 30 minutes.

Melt 1 tablespoon butter in large non-stick skillet over medium-high heat. Add spinach and stir until wilted, 3 minutes. Arrange spinach in bottom of 13 x 9 x 2-inch glass baking dish.

Melt remaining 2 tablespoons butter in heavy saucepan over medium-high heat. Add onion and sauté until tender, about 5 minutes. Add flour; stir 1 minute. Gradually whisk in mushrooms with their soaking liquid and cream. Boil until sauce thickens, whisking constantly, about 3 minutes. Mix in turkey. Season with salt and pepper.

Preheat oven to 400°F. Crack eggs open over spinach, spacing evenly. Spoon turkey mixture around eggs, leaving yolks exposed. Sprinkle Parmesan over. Bake until eggs are just set, 15 minutes. Serve with bread.

*Available at Italian markets, specialty foods stores and many supermarkets.*

ABOVE: CHICKEN, CORN AND NOODLE SOUP WITH SAFFRON. BELOW: EGGS FLORENTINE PLUS.

# HALLOWEEN

Listen up, boys and ghouls: Your night to howl has arrived. As the moon rises white and waxy and black trees shake bony limbs free of the last dead leaves, sensible people ought to be safe and snug at home. So why then (a moment of complete madness?) have you just invited 20 gobbling goblins over for a little devilish fun, when you should be in bed with the blankets pulled over your head?

Chalk it up to a second childhood. As kids, the best part about being scared by a ghost made of worn-out sheets was the laugh of relief enjoyed afterward. As grown-ups, giggling at the spooky fun is still the main event. Only the menu has changed. Where once a caramel apple, a popcorn ball and a lifetime supply of miniature Tootsie Rolls was all we could ever want, now we hunger for more serious, or at least savory, fare. That's where this bewitching Halloween party comes in. The silly fun extends only as far as the names of the dishes: The food is hearty and real, no illusion, and very definitely a treat.

Opposite (clockwise from top left): Dem Rattlin' Bones; Creepy Crawlers with Spicy Mayonnaise; and Tombstone Taters.

## Séance Spirits

*Guaranteed to warm even the chilliest of bones. This rendition of hot apple cider (below) is made more grown-up with a hearty spike of applejack. For youngsters, make a second batch, omitting the alcohol.*

**20 servings**

| | |
|---|---|
| 20 | WHOLE CLOVES |
| 1 | LARGE ORANGE |
| 5 | QUARTS APPLE CIDER |
| 10 | CINNAMON STICKS |
| 2½ | CUPS APPLEJACK |
| | ADDITIONAL CINNAMON STICKS (OPTIONAL) |

Press cloves into orange. Place orange in large pot. Add cider and 10 cinnamon sticks and bring to boil. Remove from heat. Cover and steep 30 minutes. Remove orange and cinnamon sticks. *(Can be prepared 2 days ahead. Cover and chill.)* Bring to simmer. Add applejack. Ladle into mugs and serve with additional cinnamon sticks for stirrers if desired.

## Creepy Crawlers with Spicy Mayonnaise

*Shrimp are served with a mayonnaise reminiscent of remoulade, a spicy Creole sauce for cold seafood. If you live in an area where fresh crab are available, offer them alongside, too.*

**20 servings**

| | |
|---|---|
| 3 | CUPS MAYONNAISE |
| 3 | GREEN ONIONS, FINELY CHOPPED |
| ¼ | CUP CHOPPED FRESH PARSLEY |
| ¼ | CUP FRESH LEMON JUICE |
| 2 | CELERY STALKS, FINELY CHOPPED |
| 2 | TABLESPOONS FINELY CHOPPED DRAINED CAPERS |
| 1½ | TABLESPOONS CREOLE MUSTARD OR OTHER PREPARED HOT MUSTARD |
| 1 | TABLESPOON PAPRIKA |
| 1 | TEASPOON CAYENNE PEPPER |
| 1 | TEASPOON SALT |
| ½ | TEASPOON WHITE WINE VINEGAR |
| 4 | LEMONS, HALVED |
| 1 | ONION, QUARTERED |
| 4½ | POUNDS LARGE UNCOOKED SHRIMP, PEELED, DEVEINED, END TAILS LEFT INTACT |
| 4 | RED BELL PEPPERS, CUT INTO STRIPS |
| 4 | YELLOW BELL PEPPERS, CUT INTO STRIPS |

Mix first 11 ingredients in medium bowl. Cover and refrigerate until ready to use. *(Can be prepared 3 days ahead.)*

Bring large pot of water to boil. Squeeze juice from lemons into water. Add lemon halves and onion and return to boil. Add shrimp and cook until pink and firm, about 2 minutes. Drain shrimp, discarding lemons and onion. Transfer shrimp to bowl of ice water and cool. Drain well. *(Can be made 1 day ahead. Cover and chill.)*

Place mayonnaise mixture in serving bowl. Set in center of platter. Surround with shrimp and bell peppers.

## Dem Rattlin' Bones

*The sauce on these pork ribs has a nice tang. Serve the extra sauce on the side.*

**20 servings**

½ CUP VEGETABLE OIL
1 ONION, CHOPPED
12 GARLIC CLOVES, FINELY CHOPPED
4 CUPS CHILI SAUCE
2 CUPS BEER
2 CUPS WATER
1 CUP FIRMLY PACKED DARK BROWN SUGAR
3 TABLESPOONS WHITE WINE VINEGAR
2 TABLESPOONS PLUS 2 TEASPOONS DRY MUSTARD
4 TEASPOONS WORCESTERSHIRE SAUCE
2 TEASPOONS HOT PEPPER SAUCE (SUCH AS TABASCO)
7 POUNDS PORK BABY BACK RIB RACKS

Heat oil in heavy large saucepan over medium-low heat. Add onion and sauté until soft, about 8 minutes. Add garlic and sauté 1 minute. Add chili sauce, beer, water, sugar, vinegar, mustard, Worcestershire and hot pepper sauce. Bring to boil, stirring occasionally. Reduce heat and simmer until reduced to 4 cups, stirring occasionally, about 1 hour 15 minutes. Cool.

Divide ribs between 2 large baking dishes. Brush with half of sauce. Cover ribs and remaining sauce separately and refrigerate overnight.

Preheat oven to 350°F. Transfer ribs to heavy large baking sheets. Roast ribs until tender, basting frequently with some of remaining sauce, about 1 hour. Place remaining sauce in small saucepan and bring to simmer. Cut pork into individual ribs and place on platter. Serve ribs immediately, passing chili-garlic sauce separately.

## Tombstone Taters

*A baked-potato lover's dream.*

**makes 60**

60 BABY RED NEW POTATOES
1 POUND BACON SLICES, CUT CROSSWISE INTO THIN STRIPS
1½ CUPS GRATED CHEDDAR CHEESE
1 PINT SOUR CREAM
⅓ CUP CHOPPED FRESH CHIVES OR GREEN ONION TOPS

Line large baking sheet with foil. Bring large pot of salted water to boil. Add potatoes and cook until almost tender, about 8 minutes. Drain and cool. Using small sharp knife, cut thin slice off 1 end of each potato, so it stands upright. Starting at opposite end, cut out center of each potato, leaving ¼- to ½-inch-thick shell (reserve centers for another use). Place potatoes flat side down on prepared baking sheet. *(Can be prepared 1 day ahead. Cover and chill. Let stand 1 hour at room temperature before continuing.)*

Cook bacon in heavy large skillet over medium-low heat until bacon is cooked but not too crisp, about 8 minutes. Transfer bacon to paper towels using slotted spoon and drain. *(Can be prepared 2 hours ahead. Cover and let stand at room temperature.)*

Preheat oven to 400°F. Season potato shells with salt and pepper. Fill center of each potato with cheese. Bake until cheese melts and potatoes are heated through, about 10 minutes. Top each with small dollop of sour cream. Sprinkle with bacon and chives.

## Vampire Chasers

*Onions, leeks and garlic are sure to keep even the most voracious vampires at bay. But don't let this warning scare you off—the ingredients that go into the topping for these toasts are cooked together slowly until their natural sweetness emerges.*

**makes 60**

7 LARGE LEEKS (WHITE AND PALE GREEN PARTS ONLY)
6 TABLESPOONS (¾ STICK) UNSALTED BUTTER
2 SMALL ONIONS, FINELY CHOPPED
7 LARGE GARLIC CLOVES, MINCED
¾ CUP DRY WHITE WINE
½ TEASPOON GROUND NUTMEG
2 FRENCH BREAD BAGUETTES, CUT INTO ¼-INCH-THICK SLICES
OLIVE OIL
3 CUPS GRATED GRUYÈRE CHEESE

Cut leeks lengthwise in half, then cut crosswise into very thin slices. Melt butter in heavy large skillet over medium-low heat. Add onions and sauté until soft, about 5 minutes. Add leeks and cook until very soft, stirring occasionally, about 15 minutes. Stir in garlic and sauté 2 minutes. Add wine and cook until almost no liquid remains in skillet, stirring frequently, about 6 minutes. Mix in nutmeg. Season to taste with salt and pepper. *(Can be prepared 1 day ahead. Cover and refrigerate. Bring to room temperature before using.)*

Preheat oven to 425°F. Place baguette slices on baking sheet. Brush lightly with oil. Bake until golden brown, about 6 minutes. Cool completely. *(Can be prepared 1 day ahead. Store airtight at room temperature.)*

Preheat oven to 400°F. Arrange toasts on baking sheets. Spread 1 scant tablespoon onion mixture over each. Sprinkle with Gruyère cheese. Bake until cheese bubbles, about 5 minutes. Transfer to platter and serve.

## Peanut-Butter-Cup Cupcakes

*An homage to an all-time favorite candy. Rich chocolate icing tops a moist little chocolate cake that has a creamy peanut butter center.*

**makes 30**

### CUPCAKES

2¾ CUPS ALL PURPOSE FLOUR

1 CUP UNSWEETENED COCOA POWDER

1 TABLESPOON BAKING SODA

¾ CUP (1½ STICKS) UNSALTED BUTTER, ROOM TEMPERATURE

2¼ CUPS SUGAR

3 LARGE EGGS

2 TEASPOONS VANILLA EXTRACT

2¼ CUPS MILK

### FILLING

8 OUNCES CREAM CHEESE, ROOM TEMPERATURE

⅓ CUP CREAMY PEANUT BUTTER (DO NOT USE OLD-FASHIONED STYLE OR FRESHLY GROUND)

¼ CUP MILK

½ TEASPOON VANILLA EXTRACT

4 CUPS POWDERED SUGAR

### ICING

¾ CUP PLUS 2 TABLESPOONS WHIPPING CREAM

7 OUNCES SEMISWEET CHOCOLATE, CHOPPED

CHOPPED ROASTED PEANUTS

MIXED CHOCOLATE AND ORANGE SPRINKLES

**FOR CUPCAKES:** Preheat oven to 350°F. Generously butter thirty ½-cup muffin cups. Mix flour, cocoa powder and baking soda in medium bowl. Using electric mixer, cream butter and sugar in large bowl until light. Add eggs 1 at a time, beating well after each addition. Beat in vanilla extract. Add dry ingredients alternately with milk, mixing to blend. Beat on high speed until batter is light and smooth, about 2 minutes. Divide batter among prepared cups. Bake until tester inserted into centers of cupcakes comes out clean, about 25 minutes. Cool cupcakes in pans on rack 10 minutes. Turn out onto rack and cool completely.

**FOR FILLING:** Using electric mixer, beat cream cheese and peanut butter in large bowl until smooth. Beat in milk and vanilla extract. Add sugar 1 cup at a time and beat until smooth. Beat on high speed until very light and creamy, about 5 minutes.

Line cookie sheet with waxed paper. Insert small sharp knife into side of cupcake. Move knife tip horizontally to create 1-inch-wide pocket with narrow opening. Spoon filling into pastry bag fitted with small round tip. Insert tip of pastry bag into cupcake opening. Pipe filling into cupcake, filling opening. Repeat with remaining cupcakes. Place cupcakes on prepared cookie sheet. Cover and chill 30 minutes.

**FOR ICING:** Bring whipping cream to simmer in heavy medium saucepan. Reduce heat to low. Add semisweet chocolate and whisk until melted. Let stand at room temperature until cool but not set, about 30 minutes.

Dip top of 1 cupcake into icing, covering top completely. Twist and remove, allowing excess icing to fall back into pan. Place cupcake, icing side up, onto same sheet. Top with peanuts and sprinkles. Repeat with remaining cupcakes, icing, peanuts and sprinkles. Refrigerate until icing sets, about 2 hours. *(Can be prepared 1 day ahead.)*

# DECORATING

**H**alloween is kitsch, from the accordion-paper skeletons that swing in the breeze outside front doors to the strings of bat lights that glow in windows, hinting at a friendly response to the question, "Trick or treat?" within. And when it comes to decorating the Halloween table, the "trick" is to make use of all that is silly and fun.

Start with a Halloween-themed vessel (a pumpkin- or squash-shaped ceramic tureen, a cauldron) and fill it with candy. Decorate it with dangling earrings shaped like witches, bats and ghosts and make it your centerpiece. Look for table coverings and napkins in the colors of the day: black and orange. Carve small pumpkins and squash with mad, bad or frightening faces, light them by candle and add them to the mix of things, then string lights shaped like skeletons or pumpkins around the chandelier. Now you have mood.

From there, bring on whatever Halloween collectibles you may have, whether passed down through the family, picked up at a garage sale or recently purchased at the local five-and-dime.

# THANKSGIVING

THERE ARE FOOD HOLIDAYS, AND THEN THERE IS THANKSGIVING. IT IS THE DAY OF *THE* DINNER, FOR MANY AMERICANS THE MOST IMPORTANT MEAL OF THE YEAR. ITS PLANNING AND PREPARATION, ITS CEREMONY, ITS MUCH-ANTICIPATED TASTES—NOT TO MENTION THE SHEER SIZE OF IT—ALL ADD UP TO A FEAST THAT DEFINES THE WORD, A SUPPER WORTHY OF ITS SIGNIFICANT HISTORY.

THE ORIGINAL CELEBRATION TOOK PLACE IN 1621, PROCLAIMED BY THE GOVERNOR OF THE PLYMOUTH COLONY IN COMMEMORATION OF THE PILGRIM SETTLERS' DIFFICULT FIRST YEAR IN THE NEW WORLD, AND IN GRATITUDE TO THE WAMPANOAG INDIANS FOR HELPING THE COLONY TO SURVIVE. ABRAHAM LINCOLN DECLARED THE BIG MEAL A NATIONAL HOLIDAY IN 1863.

BETWEEN THEN AND NOW, THANKSGIVING HAS SETTLED DOWN TO A FORMULA OF COMFORTABLE EXCESS, ALWAYS CENTERED AROUND A JUICY AND HANDSOMELY BROWNED TURKEY. HERE, THERE ARE THREE POSSIBLE PREPARATIONS FOR SAID BIRD, AS WELL AS ADVICE ON CARVING THE RESULTS WITHOUT LOSING YOUR COOL. STUFFING, GRAVY, CRANBERRY SAUCE, SIDE DISHES APLENTY AND ALMOST AS MANY DESSERTS ROUND OUT THIS FEAST.

OPPOSITE (CLOCKWISE FROM TOP LEFT): ROAST TURKEY WITH SAGE BUTTER; GREEN BEANS WITH ROASTED ONIONS; SPICED CRANBERRY SAUCE WITH HONEY; AND BREAD STUFFING WITH MUSHROOMS AND BACON.

## Corn and Wild Rice Soup with Smoked Sausage

*Three ingredients–corn, smoked sausage and wild rice– combine to give this appealing first-course soup (right) its sweet-spicy flavor and interesting texture. To keep things easy for the busy cook, the soup can be made up to two days ahead.*

**12 servings**

12½ CUPS (OR MORE) CANNED LOW-SALT CHICKEN BROTH

1¼ CUPS WILD RICE (ABOUT 7½ OUNCES)

6¼ CUPS FROZEN CORN KERNELS (ABOUT 2½ POUNDS), THAWED

2 TABLESPOONS VEGETABLE OIL

10 OUNCES FULLY COOKED SMOKED SAUSAGE (SUCH AS KIELBASA), CUT INTO ½-INCH CUBES

3 CARROTS, PEELED, DICED

2 MEDIUM ONIONS, CHOPPED

1½ CUPS HALF AND HALF

CHOPPED FRESH CHIVES OR PARSLEY

Bring 5 cups broth to simmer in heavy medium saucepan over medium heat. Add rice and simmer until all liquid evaporates and rice is almost tender, stirring occasionally, 40 minutes.

Meanwhile, blend 3¾ cups corn and 1½ cups chicken broth in processor until thick, almost smooth puree forms. Heat vegetable oil in heavy large Dutch oven over medium-high heat. Add sausage and sauté until beginning to brown, about 5 minutes. Add carrots and onions and stir 3 minutes. Add remaining 6 cups chicken broth and bring soup to simmer. Reduce heat to low and simmer soup for 15 minutes.

Add cooked wild rice, corn puree and remaining 2½ cups corn kernels to soup. Cook until wild rice is very tender and flavors blend, about 15 minutes longer. Mix in half and half.

Thin soup with more chicken broth, if desired. Season soup to taste with salt and pepper. *(Soup can be prepared 2 days ahead. Refrigerate until cold; cover and keep refrigerated. Rewarm soup over medium-low heat before continuing.)*

Ladle soup into bowls. Garnish with chives or parsley and serve.

## Roast Turkey with Sage Butter

*This all-American bird is embellished with a sage-and-bacon butter that gets spread under and over the skin. That same butter also flavors the rich gravy.*

**12 servings**

BUTTER

8 SLICES BACON (ABOUT ½ POUND)

1 CUP (2 STICKS) UNSALTED BUTTER, ROOM TEMPERATURE

3 TABLESPOONS CHOPPED FRESH SAGE OR 3 TEASPOONS DRIED

TURKEY AND GRAVY

1 16-POUND TURKEY

3 CUPS CHOPPED LEEKS (WHITE AND PALE GREEN PARTS ONLY; ABOUT 2 MEDIUM)

8 LARGE FRESH SAGE SPRIGS

3 BAY LEAVES, CRUMBLED

4½ CUPS (ABOUT) CANNED LOW-SALT CHICKEN BROTH

FRESH SAGE AND PARSLEY SPRIGS

**FOR BUTTER:** Cook bacon in heavy large skillet over medium heat until brown and crisp. Transfer bacon to paper towels and drain. Crumble bacon finely. Mix butter, sage and bacon in medium bowl. Season lightly with salt and pepper. *(Can be made 2 days ahead. Cover and chill. Bring to room temperature before using.)*

**FOR TURKEY AND GRAVY:** Pat turkey dry with paper towels. Season cavity with salt and pepper. Place leeks, 8 sage sprigs and bay leaves in cavity. Slide hand under skin of turkey breast to loosen skin. Spread ⅓ cup sage butter over breast meat under skin. Place turkey on rack set in large roasting pan. Rub 2 tablespoons sage butter over outside of turkey. Set aside ⅓ cup butter for gravy; reserve remainder for basting. *(Can be made 1 day ahead. Cover; chill. Let stand at room temperature 1 hour before continuing.)*

Position rack in bottom third of oven and preheat to 350°F. Pour ⅓ cup broth over turkey. Roast turkey until thermometer inserted into thickest part of inner thigh registers 180°F, basting every 30 minutes with ⅓ cup broth and occasionally brushing with sage butter, about 3 hours. Transfer turkey to platter; tent with foil. Let stand 30 minutes.

Remove rack from pan. Pour pan juices into large glass measuring cup. Spoon off fat; discard. Pour juices back into pan. Set pan over 2 burners set on high heat. Add 2 cups broth. Boil until liquid is reduced to 2 cups, scraping up browned bits, about 10 minutes. Whisk in reserved ⅓ cup sage butter. Season gravy with pepper.

Uncover platter. Garnish with sage and parsley. Serve turkey with gravy.

## Bread Stuffing with Mushrooms and Bacon

*The turkey's flavors of bacon and sage are repeated in this robust stuffing (below). Mushrooms add a nice touch.*

**12 servings**

| | |
|---|---|
| 1¼ | POUNDS SOURDOUGH BREAD, CRUSTS TRIMMED, CUT INTO ½-INCH CUBES (12 CUPS) |
| ¾ | POUND BACON (ABOUT 12 SLICES), CUT INTO ½-INCH PIECES |
| 3 | CUPS CHOPPED LEEKS (WHITE AND PALE GREEN PARTS ONLY; ABOUT 2 MEDIUM) |
| 3 | CUPS CHOPPED CELERY |
| 1 | POUND MUSHROOMS, SLICED |
| 1½ | TABLESPOONS DRIED RUBBED SAGE |
| 2 | TEASPOONS DRIED THYME |
| 1 | TEASPOON SALT |
| ¾ | TEASPOON PEPPER |
| 2½ | CUPS (OR MORE) CANNED LOW-SALT CHICKEN BROTH |
| 2 | LARGE EGGS |
| 1½ | TEASPOONS BAKING POWDER |

Preheat oven to 325°F. Spread bread cubes on 2 baking sheets. Bake until bread cubes are dry and crisp, stirring occasionally, about 25 minutes. Transfer bread to large bowl.

Sauté bacon in heavy large skillet over medium-high heat until brown and crisp. Using slotted spoon, transfer bacon to paper towels and drain. Pour off all but ¼ cup drippings from skillet. Add chopped leeks and celery to skillet and sauté until tender and beginning to brown, about 10 minutes. Add mushrooms, sage, thyme, salt and pepper and sauté until tender, about 10 minutes. Pour mushroom mixture over bread cubes. Add bacon and toss to blend. Mix in 2 cups broth. *(Stuffing can be prepared 1 day ahead. Cover and refrigerate.)*

Preheat oven to 350°F. Butter 13 x 9 x 2-inch glass baking dish. Beat eggs and baking powder in small bowl to blend. Mix eggs into stuffing; moisten stuffing with more broth if stuffing is dry. Transfer to prepared baking dish. Bake stuffing until cooked through and golden brown on top, about 1 hour.

### Spiced Cranberry Sauce with Honey

*Honey adds a subtle sweetness to the typically tart turkey accompaniment.*

**makes 3 cups**

| | |
|---|---|
| 1¾ | CUPS CRANBERRY JUICE COCKTAIL |
| ¾ | CUP HONEY |
| 1 | TABLESPOON GRATED ORANGE PEEL |
| 1 | CINNAMON STICK |
| 1 | BAY LEAF |
| 1 | TEASPOON MINCED PEELED FRESH GINGER |
| ¾ | TEASPOON GROUND CORIANDER |
| ½ | TEASPOON COARSE SALT |
| ½ | TEASPOON PEPPER |
| 2 | WHOLE CLOVES |
| ⅛ | TEASPOON CAYENNE PEPPER |
| 1 | 12-OUNCE BAG FRESH OR FROZEN CRANBERRIES |

Combine 1½ cups cranberry juice cocktail, honey and orange peel in heavy medium saucepan. Bring mixture to simmer over medium heat, stirring until honey dissolves. Simmer 4 minutes to blend flavors. Add cinnamon stick, bay leaf, ginger, coriander, salt, pepper, cloves and cayenne pepper; simmer 2 minutes. Add cranberries and simmer until berries burst and sauce is thick, stirring occasionally, about 15 minutes. Remove from heat. Discard bay leaf; mix in remaining ¼ cup cranberry juice cocktail. Refrigerate cranberry sauce until well chilled. *(Can be prepared 3 days ahead. Cover and keep refrigerated.)*

### Potato Gratin with Mustard and Cheddar Cheese

*Here, white cheddar goes into a rich and creamy potato gratin that is a great substitute for—or, at a particularly lavish feast, a fine accompaniment to—mashed potatoes on the Thanksgiving table.*

**12 servings**

| | |
|---|---|
| 1 | TABLESPOON BUTTER |
| 1 | CUP FRESH WHITE BREADCRUMBS |
| 1 | TABLESPOON DRIED THYME |
| 2 | TEASPOONS SALT |
| 1 | TEASPOON PEPPER |
| 1 | POUND SHARP WHITE CHEDDAR CHEESE, GRATED |
| ¼ | CUP ALL PURPOSE FLOUR |
| 5 | POUNDS RUSSET POTATOES, PEELED, THINLY SLICED |
| 4 | CUPS CANNED LOW-SALT CHICKEN BROTH |
| 1 | CUP WHIPPING CREAM |
| 6 | TABLESPOONS DIJON MUSTARD |

Melt butter in heavy large skillet over medium heat. Add breadcrumbs and stir until crumbs are golden brown, about 10 minutes. Cool crumbs. *(Can be prepared 2 days ahead. Cover and let stand at room temperature.)*

Position rack in center of oven and preheat to 400°F. Butter 15 x 10 x 2-inch (4-quart) glass baking dish. Mix thyme, salt and pepper in small bowl. Combine grated cheddar cheese and flour in large bowl; toss to coat cheese. Arrange ⅓ of potatoes over bottom of prepared dish. Sprinkle ⅓ of thyme mixture, then ⅓ of cheese mixture over. Repeat layering of potatoes, thyme mixture and cheese mixture 2 more times. Whisk chicken broth, whipping cream and mustard in medium bowl to blend. Pour broth mixture over potatoes.

Bake potatoes 30 minutes. Sprinkle buttered crumbs over. Bake until potatoes are tender and top is golden brown, about 1 hour longer. Let stand 15 minutes before serving.

### Green Beans with Roasted Onions

*In this recipe, green beans are enhanced with buttery, slow-roasted onions that have been stirred into a sweetened vinegar sauce.*

**12 servings**

| | |
|---|---|
| | NONSTICK VEGETABLE OIL SPRAY |
| 6 | ONIONS (ABOUT 2½ POUNDS), PEELED, EACH CUT VERTICALLY THROUGH ROOT END INTO 12 TO 14 WEDGES |
| 6 | TABLESPOONS (¾ STICK) BUTTER |
| 2 | CUPS CANNED LOW-SALT CHICKEN BROTH |
| 3 | TABLESPOONS SUGAR |
| 2 | TABLESPOONS RED WINE VINEGAR |
| 3 | POUNDS SLENDER GREEN BEANS, ENDS TRIMMED |

Preheat oven 450°F. Spray 2 heavy large baking sheets with vegetable oil spray. Arrange onions in single layer on prepared sheets. Dot onions with 4 tablespoons butter, dividing equally. Season with salt and pepper. Bake until onions are dark brown on bottom, about 35 minutes.

Meanwhile, boil broth in heavy large skillet over high heat until reduced to ½ cup, about 6 minutes. Add sugar and vinegar and whisk until sugar dissolves and mixture comes to boil.

Add onions to sauce; reduce heat to medium-low. Simmer until liquid is slightly reduced, about 5 minutes. Season with salt and pepper. *(Can be prepared 1 day ahead. Cover and chill. Rewarm over low heat before continuing.)*

Cook green beans in large pot of boiling salted water until crisp-tender, about 5 minutes. Drain well. Return beans to same pot. Add remaining 2 tablespoons butter and toss to coat. Mound beans in large shallow bowl. Top with onion mixture and serve.

## Baked Butternut Squash with Apples and Maple Syrup

*Slices of butternut squash and green apple bake with currants and maple syrup for a terrific side dish.*

**12 servings**

2½  TO 2¾ POUNDS BUTTERNUT SQUASH (ABOUT 2 MEDIUM), PEELED, QUARTERED LENGTH-WISE, SEEDED, CUT CROSSWISE INTO ¼-INCH-THICK SLICES (ABOUT 6 CUPS)

2¼  POUNDS MEDIUM-SIZE TART GREEN APPLES (SUCH AS GRANNY SMITH), PEELED, QUARTERED, CORED, CUT CROSSWISE INTO ¼-INCH-THICK SLICES (ABOUT 6 CUPS)

¾  CUP DRIED CURRANTS

GROUND NUTMEG

¾  CUP PURE MAPLE SYRUP

¼  CUP (½ STICK) BUTTER, CUT INTO PIECES

1½  TABLESPOONS FRESH LEMON JUICE

Preheat oven to 350°F. Cook squash in large pot of boiling salted water until almost tender, about 3 minutes. Drain well. Combine squash, apples and currants in 13 x 9 x 2-inch glass baking dish. Season generously with nutmeg, salt and pepper. Combine maple syrup, butter and lemon juice in heavy small saucepan. Whisk over low heat until butter melts. Pour syrup over squash mixture and toss to coat evenly.

Bake until squash and apples are very tender, stirring occasionally, about 1 hour. Cool 5 minutes. *(Can be made 1 day ahead. Cover with foil; chill. Rewarm covered in 350°F oven about 30 minutes.)*

ABOVE: BAKED BUTTERNUT SQUASH WITH APPLES AND MAPLE SYRUP.
BELOW: GREEN BEANS WITH ROASTED ONIONS AND POTATO GRATIN WITH MUSTARD AND CHEDDAR CHEESE.

ABOVE: LEMON CUSTARD PIE. BELOW: PUMPKIN ROLL CAKE WITH TOFFEE CREAM FILLING AND CARAMEL SAUCE.

## Lemon Custard Pies

*This old-fashioned dessert is a refreshing conclusion to the grand feast.*

**makes 2 pies or 16 servings**

### FILLING

6   LARGE EGGS

1   CUP SUGAR

1   CUP FRESH LEMON JUICE

4   LARGE EGG YOLKS

2   TABLESPOONS GRATED LEMON PEEL

1   CUP (2 STICKS) UNSALTED BUTTER, CUT INTO PIECES

½   CUP HALF AND HALF

1   TEASPOON VANILLA EXTRACT

### CRUSTS

2   CUPS ALL PURPOSE FLOUR

3   TABLESPOONS POWDERED SUGAR

¼   TEASPOON SALT

½   CUP (1 STICK) CHILLED UNSALTED BUTTER, CUT INTO PIECES

3   TABLESPOONS CHILLED VEGETABLE SHORTENING, CUT INTO PIECES

6   TABLESPOONS (ABOUT) ICE WATER

WHIPPED CREAM (OPTIONAL)
LEMON SLICES (OPTIONAL)
FRESH MINT (OPTIONAL)

**FOR FILLING:** Combine first 5 ingredients in heavy large saucepan and whisk to blend. Add butter. Whisk over medium heat until filling thickens and leaves path on back of spoon when finger is drawn across, about 13 minutes (do not boil). Mix in half and half and vanilla. Whisk until filling is very thick and smooth and just begins to bubble, about 6 minutes. Transfer to bowl. Cool 15 minutes, stirring occasionally. Cover; refrigerate until very cold, about 4 hours. *(Can be prepared 3 days ahead. Keep refrigerated.)*

**FOR CRUSTS:** Mix flour, powdered sugar and salt in processor. Add butter and shortening and process using on/off turns until mixture resembles coarse meal. Add 5 tablespoons water and process until moist clumps form, adding more water by teaspoonfuls if dough is dry. Gather dough into ball; divide into 2 equal pieces. Flatten into disks. Wrap in plastic and chill until firm, about 1 hour. *(Can be made 1 day ahead. Keep chilled.)*

Preheat oven to 375°F. Roll out 1 dough disk on lightly floured surface to 12- to 13-inch round. Transfer dough to 9-inch glass pie plate. Trim overhang to ½ inch; reserve dough scraps. Fold edge of dough under and crimp decoratively. Repeat rolling with second dough disk; fit into another 9-inch glass pie plate. Freeze until firm, 10 minutes.

Line crusts with foil; fill with dried beans or pie weights. Bake crusts until sides are set, about 20 minutes. Remove foil and beans. Continue to bake until crusts are pale golden, piercing with toothpick if crusts bubble, about 12 minutes. Cool completely on racks. Maintain oven temperature.

Roll out dough scraps on floured surface to ⅛-inch thickness. Transfer to baking sheet. Bake until golden, about 10 minutes. Cool. Maintain oven temperature. Crumble pastry into small pieces; wrap in plastic and reserve at room temperature.

Spoon half of filling into each crust. Bake until filling is set in center, about 18 minutes. Cool pies. Refrigerate until cold, about 2 hours. *(Can be made 1 day ahead. Cover and keep chilled.)* Sprinkle crumbled pastry over pies. Garnish pies with whipped cream, lemon slices and mint, if desired.

## Pumpkin Roll Cake with Toffee Cream Filling and Caramel Sauce

*This pretty roll cake is an impressive alternative to the classic pumpkin pie.*

**12 servings**

### CAKE

NONSTICK VEGETABLE OIL SPRAY

| | |
|---|---|
| ¾ | CUP CAKE FLOUR |
| 1½ | TEASPOONS GROUND CINNAMON |
| 1¼ | TEASPOONS GROUND GINGER |
| ¾ | TEASPOON GROUND ALLSPICE |
| 6 | LARGE EGGS, SEPARATED |
| ⅓ | CUP SUGAR |
| ⅓ | CUP FIRMLY PACKED GOLDEN BROWN SUGAR |
| ⅔ | CUP CANNED SOLID PACK PUMPKIN |
| ⅛ | TEASPOON SALT |

POWDERED SUGAR

### FILLING

| | |
|---|---|
| 2 | TABLESPOONS DARK RUM |
| 1 | TEASPOON UNFLAVORED GELATIN |
| 1 | CUP CHILLED WHIPPING CREAM |
| 3 | TABLESPOONS POWDERED SUGAR |
| 10 | TABLESPOONS PLUS ½ CUP ENGLISH TOFFEE PIECES (OR CHOPPED ENGLISH TOFFEE CANDY; ABOUT 7 OUNCES) |

ADDITIONAL POWDERED SUGAR

| | |
|---|---|
| 1½ | CUPS PURCHASED CARAMEL SAUCE, WARMED |

**FOR CAKE:** Preheat oven to 375°F. Spray 15 x 10 x 1-inch baking sheet with vegetable oil spray. Sift flour, cinnamon, ginger and allspice into small bowl. Using electric mixer, beat egg yolks, ⅓ cup sugar and ⅓ cup brown sugar in large bowl until very thick, about 3 minutes. On low speed, beat in pumpkin, then dry ingredients. Using clean dry beaters, beat egg whites and salt in another large bowl until stiff but not dry. Fold egg whites into batter in 3 additions. Transfer to prepared pan. Bake cake until tester inserted into center comes out clean, about 15 minutes.

Place smooth (not terry cloth) kitchen towel on work surface; dust generously with powdered sugar. Cut around pan sides to loosen cake. Turn cake out onto kitchen towel. Fold towel over 1 long side of cake. Starting at 1 long side, roll up cake in towel. Arrange cake seam side down and cool completely, about 1 hour.

**FOR FILLING:** Pour 2 tablespoons rum into heavy small saucepan; sprinkle gelatin over. Let stand until gelatin softens, about 10 minutes. Stir over low heat just until gelatin dissolves. Beat chilled whipping cream and 3 tablespoons powdered sugar in large bowl until firm peaks form. Beat in gelatin mixture. Fold in 6 tablespoons English toffee pieces.

Unroll cake; sprinkle with 4 tablespoons English toffee pieces. Spread filling over. Starting at 1 long side and using kitchen towel as aid, roll up cake to enclose filling. Place cake seam side down on platter. *(Can be prepared 1 day ahead. Cover with foil and refrigerate.)*

Trim ends of cake on slight diagonal. Dust cake with powdered sugar. Spoon some of warm sauce over top of cake. Sprinkle with ½ cup toffee. To serve, cut cake crosswise into 1-inch thick slices. Pass remaining sauce.

# HOW *to* COOK *a* TURKEY

**P**ART OF THE RITUAL OF THANKSGIVING IS THE TABLE-SIDE CARVING OF THE TURKEY, A JOB MANY FIND NERVE-RACKING, EVEN TERRIFYING, BUT IS ACTUALLY QUITE STRAIGHTFORWARD. HERE, FOR BOTH THE NOVICE AND THE NERVOUS, IS A STEP-BY-STEP GUIDE THAT WILL HAVE YOU CARVING LIKE A PRO IN NO TIME.

There is nothing quite like a dry, overcooked turkey to deflate the ego of a proud Thanksgiving cook. And even though everyone dines on turkey every November, mastering its preparation can be tricky. There are many variables that play a part in cooking the perfect holiday bird, but following a few basic guidelines on times and weights will help ensure a moist, delicious result.

Below are approximate cooking times for different sizes of turkeys. These times are based on roasting the turkey in a 325°F oven. Some recipes call for a higher temperature for the first 30 to 45 minutes, and some recipes call for a 350°F oven, so the overall cooking time for those turkeys will be reduced. A good rule is to check for doneness about 30 minutes before you expect the turkey to be finished. Remember that the turkey is fully cooked when a thermometer inserted into the thickest part of the thigh (without touching bone) registers 180°F.

| TURKEY COOKING TIMES (325°F oven) | | |
|---|---|---|
| WEIGHT | UNSTUFFED | STUFFED |
| 10 to 18 pounds | 3 to 3½ hours | 3¾ to 4½ hours |
| 18 to 22 pounds | 3½ to 4 hours | 4 to 5 hours |
| 22 to 24 pounds | 4 to 4½ hours | 4½ to 5½ hours |
| 24 to 29 pounds | 4½ to 5 hours | 5½ to 6¼ hours |

# HOW *to* CARVE *a* TURKEY

**1** BEGIN CARVING THE TURKEY BY REMOVING EACH LEG. ARRANGE THE TURKEY BREAST SIDE UP ON A CUTTING BOARD. STEADY THE TURKEY WITH A CARVING FORK. CUT THE SKIN BETWEEN THE THIGH AND BREAST.

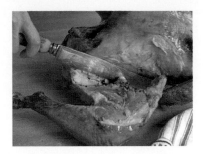

**2** NEXT, USING A LARGE KNIFE AS AN AID, PRESS THE THIGH OUTWARD TO FIND THE HIP JOINT. SLICE DOWN THROUGH THE JOINT AND REMOVE THE LEG. (ALTERNATIVELY, YOU CAN GRASP THE LEG, TWIST IT AT THE JOINT AND REMOVE.)

**3** CUT BETWEEN THE THIGH BONE AND DRUMSTICK BONE TO DIVIDE THE LEG INTO ONE THIGH PIECE AND ONE DRUMSTICK.

**4** TO CARVE THE DRUMSTICK, STEADY IT WITH A CARVING FORK AND CUT A THICK SLICE OF MEAT FROM ONE SIDE OF THE DRUMSTICK, ALONG THE BONE.

**5** NEXT, TURN THE DRUMSTICK OVER SO THAT THE CUT SIDE FACES DOWN. CUT OFF ANOTHER THICK SLICE OF MEAT. REPEAT, TURNING THE DRUMSTICK ONTO A FLAT SIDE AND CUTTING OFF MEAT, CARVING A TOTAL OF FOUR THICK SLICES.

**6** TO SLICE THE THIGH, PLACE IT FLAT SIDE DOWN ON CUTTING BOARD. STEADY THE THIGH WITH A CARVING FORK. USING THE KNIFE, CUT PARALLEL TO THE BONE AND SLICE OFF THE MEAT.

**7** BEFORE THE BREAST IS CARVED, THE WING MUST BE REMOVED. SLICE DIAGONALLY DOWN THROUGH THE BOTTOM EDGE OF THE BREAST TOWARD THE WING. USING THE KNIFE AS AN AID, PRESS THE WING OUT TO FIND THE SHOULDER JOINT; CUT THROUGH THE JOINT AND REMOVE THE WING.

**8** TO CARVE THE BREAST MEAT, HOLD THE BACK OF THE CARVING FORK AGAINST THE BREASTBONE. STARTING PARALLEL TO THE BREASTBONE, SLICE DIAGONALLY THROUGH THE MEAT. LIFT OFF EACH SLICE, HOLDING IT BETWEEN THE KNIFE AND FORK.

**9** CONTINUE UNTIL YOU HAVE CARVED ALL THE MEAT ON ONE SIDE OF THE BREAST. REPEAT CARVING ON THE OTHER SIDE OF THE BREAST.

# VARIATIONS *on the* TURKEY THEME

I'T'S THE ENDURING SYMBOL OF NATIONAL CELEBRATION. IT'S AN ORGANIC CENTERPIECE FOR THE HOLIDAY TABLE. IT'S A GENEROUS PROVIDER, FEEDING THE WHOLE FAMILY AND ALL THE WAIFS AND STRAYS AS WELL. BEST OF ALL, IT TASTES GREAT.

THANKSGIVING JUST WOULDN'T BE, WELL, THANKSGIVING WITHOUT TURKEY. BUT THIS DOESN'T MEAN IT HAS TO BE THE SAME TURKEY YEAR AFTER YEAR. THE TWO RECIPES HERE ARE STEEPED IN TRADITION, BUT EACH ADDS A NEW TWIST TO TURKEY PREPARATION—AND A WONDERFUL GRAVY, TOO.

## Roast Turkey with Maple Herb Butter and Gravy

**12 servings**

### TURKEY

| | |
|---|---|
| 2 | CUPS APPLE CIDER |
| ⅓ | CUP PURE MAPLE SYRUP |
| 2 | TABLESPOONS CHOPPED FRESH THYME OR 2 TEASPOONS DRIED |
| 2 | TABLESPOONS CHOPPED FRESH MARJORAM OR 2 TEASPOONS DRIED |
| 1½ | TEASPOONS GRATED LEMON PEEL |
| ¾ | CUP (1½ STICKS) BUTTER, ROOM TEMPERATURE |
| 1 | 14-POUND TURKEY, NECK AND GIBLETS RESERVED |
| 2 | CUPS CHOPPED ONION |
| 1½ | CUPS CHOPPED CELERY WITH LEAVES |
| 1 | CUP COARSELY CHOPPED CARROT |
| 2 | CUPS CANNED LOW-SALT CHICKEN BROTH |

### GRAVY

| | |
|---|---|
| 3 | CUPS (ABOUT) CANNED LOW-SALT CHICKEN BROTH |
| 3 | TABLESPOONS ALL PURPOSE FLOUR |
| 1 | TEASPOON CHOPPED FRESH THYME OR ½ TEASPOON DRIED |
| 1 | SMALL BAY LEAF |
| 2 | TABLESPOONS APPLE BRANDY (OPTIONAL) |

**FOR TURKEY:** Boil apple cider and maple syrup in heavy large saucepan over medium-high heat until reduced to ½ cup, about 20 minutes. Remove from heat. Mix in half of chopped thyme, half of marjoram and 1½ teaspoons lemon peel. Add butter and whisk until melted. Season generously with salt and pepper. Cover and refrigerate until cold, about 2 hours. *(Can be prepared 2 days ahead. Keep refrigerated.)*

Position rack in lowest third of oven and preheat to 375°F. Pat turkey dry with paper towels. Place turkey on rack set in large roasting pan. Slide hand under skin of turkey breast to loosen skin. Rub ½ cup maple butter over breast skin. If stuffing turkey, spoon stuffing into main cavity. Rub ¼ cup maple butter over outside of turkey. Reserve remaining maple butter for gravy. Tie legs together loosely to hold shape of turkey. Arrange onion, celery, carrot and reserved turkey neck and giblets around turkey in pan. Sprinkle vegetables with remaining 1 tablespoon thyme and remaining 1 tablespoon marjoram. Pour 2 cups broth into pan.

Roast turkey 30 minutes. Reduce oven temperature to 350°F. Cover entire turkey loosely with heavy-duty foil and roast until meat thermometer inserted into thickest part of thigh registers 180°F or until juices run clear when thickest part of thigh is pierced with skewer, basting occasionally with pan juices, about 2 hours 25 minutes for unstuffed turkey (2 hours 55 minutes for stuffed turkey). Transfer turkey to platter. Tent turkey with aluminum foil and let stand 30 minutes; reserve mixture in pan for gravy.

**FOR GRAVY:** Strain pan juices into large measuring cup, pressing on solids with back of spoon. Spoon fat from pan juices. Add enough chicken broth to pan juices to measure 3 cups. Transfer liquid to heavy medium saucepan and bring to boil. Mix 3 tablespoons reserved maple butter and flour in small bowl to form smooth paste. Whisk paste into broth mixture. Add chopped fresh thyme and bay leaf. Boil until reduced to sauce consistency, whisking occasionally, about 10 minutes. Mix in apple brandy, if desired. Season gravy to taste with salt and pepper.

Brush turkey with any remaining maple butter and serve with gravy.

## Southwestern Turkey with Garlic-Ancho Chili Paste and Gravy

**14 servings**

### PASTE

3 LARGE HEADS GARLIC

3 LARGE DRIED ANCHO CHILIES,* RINSED, STEMMED, SEEDED, TORN INTO PIECES

½ CUP CORN OIL

1½ TEASPOONS GROUND CUMIN

½ TEASPOON HONEY

### TURKEY

1 17- TO 18-POUND TURKEY, NECK AND GIBLETS RESERVED

2 TABLESPOONS CORN OIL

1½ POUNDS TURKEY NECKS OR WINGS, CUT INTO 1-INCH PIECES

1 LARGE ONION, CHOPPED

3 CELERY STALKS, CHOPPED

1 LARGE TOMATO, CHOPPED

1 TEASPOON ALLSPICE BERRIES

5 CUPS CANNED LOW-SALT CHICKEN BROTH

### GRAVY

2 CUPS (ABOUT) CANNED LOW-SALT CHICKEN BROTH

6 TABLESPOONS ALL PURPOSE FLOUR

CAYENNE PEPPER

**FOR PASTE:** Preheat oven to 350°F. Separate heads of garlic into individual cloves (do not peel). Pierce each clove once with toothpick. Scatter garlic on baking sheet; roast until tender and beginning to brown, about 25 minutes. Cool 5 minutes. Peel garlic, cutting hard tip off each clove. Pack enough garlic into ½-cup measuring cup to fill (about 40 cloves); reserve any remaining garlic. Blend ½ cup garlic in processor to form coarse puree.

Meanwhile, place chilies in small saucepan. Add enough water just to cover. Simmer over medium-low heat until chilies are soft and most of water evaporates, about 15 minutes. Add chili mixture, oil, cumin and honey to garlic in processor. Puree until smooth. Season with salt and pepper. *(Can be made 1 week ahead. Cover paste and garlic separately and refrigerate.)*

**FOR TURKEY:** Pat turkey dry. Season with salt and pepper. Slide hand under skin of turkey breast to loosen skin. Spread ½ cup garlic-chili paste over breast under skin. If stuffing turkey, spoon stuffing into main cavity. Rub 2 tablespoons paste all over outside of turkey. Reserve remaining paste for gravy. Tie legs together loosely to hold shape of turkey. Place on rack set in roasting pan. *(Can be prepared 1 day ahead if turkey is not stuffed. Chill turkey and paste separately.)*

Position rack in lowest third of oven and preheat to 325°F. Heat 2 tablespoons oil in heavy large skillet over high heat. Add neck and giblets, turkey neck pieces and onion; sauté until brown, about 15 minutes. Place contents of skillet around turkey in pan.

Add celery, tomato, allspice and any reserved garlic to pan; pour in 2 cups broth. Roast turkey 1 hour 30 minutes. Tent turkey and entire pan loosely with heavy-duty foil. Continue to roast turkey until meat thermometer inserted into thickest part of thigh registers 180°F or until juices run clear when thickest part of thigh is pierced with skewer, basting often with pan juices and 3 cups broth, about 1 hour 40 minutes longer for unstuffed turkey (about 2 hours 25 minutes longer for stuffed turkey). Place turkey on platter. Tent with foil; let stand at least 30 minutes. Reserve mixture in pan for gravy.

**FOR GRAVY:** Using tongs, remove turkey parts from pan; discard. Pour mixture in pan into sieve set over large bowl. Press on solids in sieve to release pan juices. Spoon fat from pan juices; add enough chicken broth to pan juices to measure 6 cups.

Stir ½ cup reserved garlic-chili paste in heavy large saucepan over medium-high heat until liquefied. Add flour and stir 1 minute (mixture will be very thick). Gradually add 6 cups broth mixture, whisking until smooth. Simmer until reduced to 4½ cups, about 20 minutes. Season with cayenne, salt and pepper.

Serve turkey with gravy.

*\*Available at Latin American markets and specialty foods stores.*

# HANUKKAH

Among Jewish holidays, Hanukkah, the Festival of Lights, is one of the happiest. Commemorating the defeat of Antiochus of Syria by the Maccabees over two thousand years ago, it also celebrates the miracle of the synagogue lamps, which burned for eight days and nights on a one day's supply of oil. The menorah, one new candle of which is lit each night of the eight-day holiday, symbolizes the miracle, as does the tradition of serving the potato pancakes called latkes and dessert fritters, both fried in oil. Other traditions include the exchanging of gifts and games of dreidel, both of which make the holiday a magical one for children.

Beyond latkes (turn to page 124 for four delicious versions of the classic recipe) and fritters, the Hanukkah menu varies with the country of the cook. Those who trace their ancestry to the countries around the Mediterranean Sea will recognize the menu here, which explores the tastes of the Sephardic tradition. It makes a delicious meal to celebrate the holiday .

Opposite: Braised Lamb in Pomegranate Sauce and Seven-Vegetable Couscous with Chunky Onion Harissa.

## Roasted Eggplant and Pepper Salad with Pita Bread and Sesame Spread

**8 servings**

NONSTICK VEGETABLE OIL SPRAY
2    EGGPLANTS (ABOUT
     2½ POUNDS TOTAL), CUT INTO
     3 x ¾ x ¾-INCH STRIPS
2    LARGE GREEN BELL PEPPERS,
     CUT INTO ½-INCH-WIDE STRIPS
2    LARGE RED BELL PEPPERS, CUT
     INTO ½-INCH WIDE STRIPS
8    LARGE GARLIC CLOVES
     (UNPEELED)
½    CUP OLIVE OIL

¾    CUP RED WINE VINEGAR
1    TABLESPOON GROUND CUMIN
1½   TEASPOONS SALT
1½   TEASPOONS PEPPER
⅜    TEASPOON CAYENNE PEPPER

8    WARM PITA BREAD ROUNDS,
     CUT INTO WEDGES
     SESAME SPREAD
     (SEE RECIPE AT RIGHT)

Position rack in top third of oven and preheat to 450°F. Spray heavy large baking sheet with nonstick vegetable oil spray. Combine eggplant, peppers, garlic and oil in large bowl. Toss well. Transfer to prepared sheet. Bake until eggplant is brown and vegetables are tender, stirring every 10 minutes, about 50 minutes. Remove garlic and reserve. Scrape vegetables and all pan juices into bowl.

Combine vinegar, cumin, salt, pepper and cayenne in processor. Peel roasted garlic; add to processor. Puree until smooth. Toss vegetable mixture with ¼ cup garlic dressing. Cool, tossing occasionally. *(Can be made 1 day ahead. Cover and refrigerate vegetables and remaining garlic dressing separately. Bring to room temperature.)*

Mound salad in center of large platter. Surround with pita wedges. Serve, passing remaining dressing and Sesame Spread separately.

## Sesame Spread

*Kosher dietary laws forbid eating dairy products with meats. So margarine, instead of butter, is used in the spread.*

**makes about 1¼ cups**

1    CUP (2 STICKS) UNSALTED
     PAREVE MARGARINE,*
     ROOM TEMPERATURE
⅔    CUP TOASTED SESAME SEEDS
1    TEASPOON SALT

Beat margarine, sesame seeds and salt to blend in small bowl. *(Can be prepared 2 days ahead. Cover and refrigerate. Bring to room temperature before serving.)*

*\*A nondairy margarine available at most supermarkets across the country.*

OPPOSITE: ROASTED EGGPLANT AND PEPPER SALAD WITH PITA BREAD AND SESAME SPREAD.

# HOW *to* MAKE BLINTZES *for* HANUKKAH

**E**VER SINCE THE FIRST FESTIVAL OF LIGHTS WAS CELEBRATED MORE THAN TWO THOUSAND YEARS AGO, DAIRY PRODUCTS AND OIL-COOKED FOODS HAVE BEEN HONORED ELEMENTS OF THE HANUKKAH TABLE. HERE, THEY ARE BROUGHT TOGETHER BEAUTIFULLY IN DELICATE BLINTZES. FILLED WITH A SWEETENED CHEESE MIXTURE, LIGHTLY FRIED AND TOPPED WITH A LUSCIOUS MIXED-BERRY COMPOTE, THEY MAKE A PERFECT TREAT FOR THE HOLIDAY.

## Cheese Blintzes with Three-Berry Compote

*A blintz is simply a filled crepe. For those new to the art of crepe-making, there is plenty of batter here to allow for a few practice crepes. The completed blintzes can be frozen for a month.*

**makes 13**

### FILLING

| | |
|---|---|
| 1¼ | POUNDS HOOP CHEESE OR 2 POUNDS NONFAT COTTAGE CHEESE |
| ½ | CUP PLUS 1 TABLESPOON SUGAR |
| 2 | EXTRA-LARGE EGGS |
| ½ | TEASPOON (SCANT) SALT |

### CREPES

| | |
|---|---|
| 1½ | CUPS WATER |
| 3 | EXTRA-LARGE EGGS |
| 1½ | CUPS SIFTED ALL PURPOSE FLOUR |
| 1 | TABLESPOON SUGAR |
| ¾ | TEASPOON SALT |

VEGETABLE OIL

### COMPOTE

| | |
|---|---|
| 2½ | CUPS FROZEN UNSWEETENED BOYSENBERRIES (ABOUT 11 OUNCES) |
| 2½ | CUPS FROZEN UNSWEETENED BLUEBERRIES (ABOUT 11 OUNCES) |
| 1 | 12-OUNCE BASKET STRAWBERRIES, HULLED, HALVED |
| 1 | CUP SUGAR |
| 1 | TEASPOON GRATED LEMON PEEL |
| 1½ | TABLESPOONS CORNSTARCH |
| | FRESH LEMON JUICE (OPTIONAL) |

VEGETABLE OIL
SOUR CREAM
LEMON PEEL STRIPS (OPTIONAL)

**FOR FILLING:** If using cottage cheese, place in center of kitchen towel, gather towel around cheese and squeeze to remove excess moisture. Measure 2½ cups packed cottage cheese (reserve remainder for another use). Combine 1¼ pounds hoop cheese or 2½ cups packed dry cottage cheese and sugar in processor; blend well. Add eggs and salt; process until almost smooth, scraping down sides of bowl occasionally. Transfer to bowl. Cover and refrigerate. *(Can be made 1 day ahead.)*

**FOR CREPES:** Combine 1½ cups water and eggs in blender. Add flour, sugar and salt. Blend on low speed until very smooth, stopping occasionally to scrape down sides of container. Pour batter into medium bowl. Let stand at room temperature at least 1 hour and up to 2 hours, stirring occasionally.

Heat 10-inch nonstick skillet over high heat. Brush very lightly with oil. Transfer 3 tablespoons batter to small cup. Working quickly, pour batter into center of skillet; tilt and shake skillet to spread batter into 7-inch round. Reduce heat to medium-high and cook crepe until bottom is speckled brown, about 45 seconds. Loosen sides of crepe with spatula and turn out onto paper towel cooked side up. Cover with paper towel. Repeat with remaining batter, brushing pan occasionally with oil and layering crepes between paper towels.

Place 1 crepe cooked side up on work surface. Place ¼ cup filling in 3-inch-long log just below center. Fold bottom of crepe over filling. Fold sides in. Roll crepe up, enclosing filling completely. Transfer blintz to plastic-lined platter. Repeat with remaining filling and crepes. *(Can be prepared ahead. Cover and chill overnight or freeze up to 1 month. Do not thaw frozen blintzes before cooking.)*

**FOR COMPOTE:** Combine all berries, sugar and lemon peel in large bowl. Let stand at room temperature until berries defrost, sugar dissolves and juices form in bowl, stirring occasionally, about 1½ hours.

Strain berry mixture thoroughly, reserving juices. Place cornstarch in heavy medium saucepan. Gradually add reserved juices to cornstarch, whisking until smooth. Whisk over high heat until syrup boils and is thick and clear, about 2 minutes. Transfer to bowl. Cool 15 minutes. Mix berries into syrup. Adjust tartness with lemon juice. *(Can be prepared 3 hours ahead. Cover and refrigerate.)*

Pour oil into 2 large nonstick skillets to depth of scant ⅛ inch; heat over medium-low heat until hot. Place blintzes seam side down in skillets. Cook until bottoms are brown and crisp, shaking pans gently and moving blintzes occasionally to prevent sticking, about 6 minutes (for frozen blintzes, cover skillet for first 6 minutes). Using spatula, turn blintzes over; cook until bottoms are brown and crisp and blintzes feel firm when lightly pressed, about 5 minutes. Transfer to paper towel-lined platter. Place 2 blintzes on each plate. Spoon compote over blintzes. Top with sour cream. Sprinkle with lemon peel.

1   CREPE BATTER IS SPOONED INTO A SMALL CUP AND THEN POURED ALL AT ONCE INTO THE CENTER OF AN OILED NONSTICK SKILLET SET OVER HIGH HEAT.

2   THE SKILLET IS IMMEDIATELY TILTED AND SHAKEN TO SPREAD THE BATTER INTO A SEVEN-INCH ROUND. IT'S IMPORTANT TO WORK QUICKLY TO PRODUCE A CREPE OF UNIFORM THICKNESS.

3   CREPE IS COOKED UNTIL THE BOTTOM IS SPECKLED BROWN, ABOUT 45 SECONDS. A SPATULA IS THEN USED TO LOOSEN THE CREPE BEFORE IT IS TURNED OUT ONTO A PAPER TOWEL.

4   TO STUFF THE CREPE, ¼ CUP OF CHEESE FILLING IS FORMED INTO A THREE-INCH-LONG LOG JUST BELOW CENTER OF THE COOKED SIDE OF CREPE.

5   NEXT, BOTTOM OF CREPE IS FOLDED OVER FILLING. SIDES OF CREPE ARE THEN FOLDED IN AND CREPE IS ROLLED UP TO ENCLOSE THE FILLING COMPLETELY.

6   BLINTZES ARE COOKED SEAM SIDE DOWN UNTIL BOTTOMS ARE BROWN (SKILLET IS SHAKEN GENTLY TO PREVENT STICKING). BLINTZES ARE TURNED OVER, THEN COOKED UNTIL FIRM WHEN PRESSED.

# NEW TAKES *on a* HANUKKAH CLASSIC

**H**OT, CRISPY, EARTHY AND SUBSTANTIAL, LATKES ARE A FAVORITE WITH MANY AMONG ALL THE WONDERFUL FOODS OF THE JEWISH HOLIDAYS. WHETHER SERVED WITH SOUR CREAM OR APPLESAUCE, AS A FIRST COURSE, MAIN COURSE OR SIDE DISH, THEY ARE ALWAYS DELICIOUS AND ANTICIPATED.

WHAT MANY COOKS MAY NOT KNOW, HOWEVER, IS THAT LATKES DON'T HAVE TO BE MADE ONLY WITH POTATOES. MANY JEWS OF EASTERN EUROPEAN ANCESTRY AND MANY SEPHARDIC JEWS MAKE THEIR LATKES WITH OTHER KINDS OF VEGETABLES, INCLUDING CARROTS, PUMPKIN, ZUCCHINI, CAULIFLOWER AND SPINACH. WITH THIS IN MIND, HERE ARE SEVERAL NEW RECIPES FOR AN OLD FAVORITE.

## Classic Potato Latkes

*The secret to crisp latkes is the removal of as much liquid as possible from the ground potatoes. Serve these plain (they're a fine accompaniment to a roast with gravy), or with sour cream or applesauce.*

**makes about 18**

| | |
|---|---|
| 2 | POUNDS RUSSET POTATOES, PEELED, DICED |
| 1 | LARGE ONION, PEELED, DICED |
| 1 | EGG |
| 3 | TABLESPOONS ALL PURPOSE FLOUR |
| 1¼ | TEASPOONS SALT |
| ¾ | TEASPOON PEPPER |
| ½ | TEASPOON BAKING POWDER |
| 10 | TABLESPOONS (ABOUT) VEGETABLE OIL |

Preheat oven to 325°F. Place 2 baking sheets in oven. Line large bowl with towel. Finely grind potatoes and onion in processor (do not puree). Transfer to towel. Fold towel up around mixture; twist top, squeezing out all liquid into bowl. Let liquid stand 5 minutes. Pour off liquid, reserving any potato starch in bowl. Add potato mixture to bowl. Mix in egg, flour, salt, pepper and baking powder.

Heat 6 tablespoons oil in large skillet over medium-high heat. Working in batches, drop 1 heaping tablespoon batter per pancake into hot oil. Using back of spoon, spread to 2½- to 3-inch rounds. Cook until brown, about 3 minutes per side. Transfer to baking sheets in oven. Repeat with remaining batter, spooning off any liquid from surface of batter and adding more oil to skillet by tablespoonfuls as necessary. Serve latkes hot.

## Garden Vegetable Latkes

*Carrots, parsnips, green onions and dill make the difference in these colorful pancakes (opposite). Mix some chopped fresh dill and green onions into sour cream to pass alongside.*

### makes about 12

8 OUNCES YUKON GOLD POTATOES, PEELED, CUT INTO 1-INCH PIECES

8 OUNCES CARROTS (ABOUT 2 LARGE), PEELED, CUT INTO 1-INCH PIECES

8 OUNCES PARSNIPS (ABOUT 2 LARGE), PEELED, CUT INTO 1-INCH PIECES

¼ CUP ALL PURPOSE FLOUR

¼ CUP CHOPPED FRESH DILL

¼ CUP CHOPPED GREEN ONIONS

½ TEASPOON SALT

½ TEASPOON PEPPER

2 LARGE EGGS, BEATEN TO BLEND

10 TABLESPOONS (ABOUT) VEGETABLE OIL

Preheat oven to 325°F. Place baking sheet in oven. Using food processor fitted with medium grating disk, shred potatoes, carrots and parsnips. Place towel on work surface. Spread vegetables over. Roll up towel; squeeze tightly to absorb moisture from vegetables. Blend flour, dill, onions, salt and pepper in large bowl. Add vegetables; toss to coat. Mix in eggs.

Heat 6 tablespoons oil in large skillet over medium heat. Working in batches, drop 2 heaping tablespoons batter per pancake into hot oil. Using spoon, spread to 4-inch rounds. Cook until brown, about 3 minutes per side. Transfer to sheet in oven. Repeat with remaining batter, adding more oil to skillet by tablespoonfuls as necessary. Serve latkes hot.

## Yam Latkes with Mustard Seeds and Curry

*These innovative latkes are great as a first course, side dish or entrée. Complement them with chutney and yogurt.*

### makes about 12

2 CUPS (PACKED) COARSELY GRATED PEELED YAMS (RED-SKINNED SWEET POTATOES; ABOUT 8 OUNCES)

½ CUP CHOPPED RED BELL PEPPER

3 TABLESPOONS CORNSTARCH

1 15- TO 16-OUNCE CAN GARBANZO BEANS (CHICKPEAS), WELL DRAINED

1 LARGE EGG

2 TEASPOONS CURRY POWDER

1 TEASPOON SALT

¼ CUP CHOPPED CILANTRO

2 TEASPOONS MUSTARD SEEDS

8 TABLESPOONS (ABOUT) VEGETABLE OIL

Combine yams and bell pepper in large bowl. Add cornstarch; toss to coat. Puree garbanzo beans in processor to coarse paste. Add egg, curry powder and salt and blend. Transfer mixture to small bowl. Mix in cilantro and mustard seeds. Stir garbanzo bean mixture into yam mixture.

Preheat oven to 325°F. Place baking sheet in oven. Heat 6 tablespoons oil in large skillet over medium heat. Working in batches, drop 1 heaping tablespoon batter per pancake into hot oil. Using back of spoon, spread to 3-inch rounds. Cook until brown, about 3 minutes per side. Transfer to baking sheet in oven. Repeat with remaining batter, spooning off any liquid from surface of batter and adding more oil to skillet by tablespoonfuls as necessary. Serve latkes hot.

## Potato, Artichoke and Feta Cheese Latkes

*For a nice vegetarian meal, offer these with a Greek salad. Stir chopped mint into yogurt to have with the latkes.*

### makes about 12

1½ POUNDS RED-SKINNED POTATOES

1 9-OUNCE PACKAGE FROZEN ARTICHOKE HEARTS, THAWED, DICED, PATTED DRY

⅔ CUP CHOPPED LEEK (WHITE AND PALE GREEN PARTS ONLY)

½ CUP FRESHLY GRATED PARMESAN CHEESE

1 LARGE EGG, BEATEN TO BLEND

2 TABLESPOONS CHOPPED FRESH MINT

2 TEASPOONS DRIED OREGANO

1 TEASPOON SALT

½ TEASPOON PEPPER

6 OUNCES FETA CHEESE, DICED

1½ CUPS (ABOUT) FRESH FRENCH BREADCRUMBS

8 TABLESPOONS (ABOUT) OLIVE OIL

Cook potatoes in pot of boiling salted water until just tender, about 20 minutes. Drain. Cool completely and peel.

Preheat oven to 325°F. Place baking sheet in oven. Using hand grater, coarsely grate potatoes into large bowl. Add artichokes and leek. Mix Parmesan, egg, mint, oregano, salt and pepper in small bowl. Add to potatoes. Stir in feta and enough breadcrumbs to form mixture that holds together. Press ½ cup mixture into 3½-inch round. Repeat with remaining mixture.

Heat 6 tablespoons oil in large skillet over medium heat. Place 4 pancakes into skillet. Cook until brown, about 6 minutes per side. Transfer to sheet in oven. Repeat with remaining pancakes, adding more oil as necessary.

# CHRISTMAS

Christmas is such a jam-packed holiday that it can seem like a year's worth of good times, all rolled up in about two dazzling weeks. Sacred and secular, solemn and merry, it is the ultimate celebration, a glittering whirlwind of parties and meals, large and small. A happy and slightly exhausted glow of satisfaction is the mark of a successful host, one who has entertained with style and grace, sharing the good times with loved ones while loving it all. Because no Christmas can be merry if you have not had as good a time as your guests.

To that end, we suggest a range of Christmas entertainments, and encourage you to select among them with an eye towards the possible, doing just as much and no more than makes you happy and comfortable. There are three menus here, from a casual tree-trimming buffet to a simple Christmas morning breakfast to a pull-out-all-the-stops dinner. There are cookies to bake and gifts of food to make. And whether you recreate one or all of these Christmas experiences, you will be giving yourself the best gift of all: a great time in the kitchen and at the table.

# CHRISTMAS TREE-TRIMMING BUFFET *for* TWELVE

EGGNOG

SALTED ALMONDS

HONEY-GLAZED HAM *with* CRANBERRY-SHALLOT RELISH

UPSCALE MACARONI *and* CHEESE

BRUSSELS SPROUTS SALAD *with* LEMON-THYME VINAIGRETTE

CORN BREAD *with* SUN-DRIED TOMATOES

RED *and* WHITE WINES

FRUITCAKE BROWNIES

CHRISTMAS COOKIES

## Cranberry-Shallot Relish

*Make a purchased honey-glazed ham the centerpiece of your menu, then round out the buffet with delicious accompaniments; this sweet and spicy relish flavored with Marsala and ginger is just one of them. It's the perfect partner for the ham, and it's also good with roast pork, chicken or turkey. Start the evening with your favorite eggnog laced with cream Sherry, and serve salted almonds with it.*

**makes about 5 cups**

| | |
|---|---|
| 3 | TABLESPOONS VEGETABLE OIL |
| 12 | OUNCES SHALLOTS, CHOPPED |
| 1½ | CUPS SWEET MARSALA OR PORT |
| ¾ | CUP SUGAR |
| 2 | 12-OUNCE PACKAGES CRANBERRIES |
| 1 | TEASPOON CURRY POWDER |
| ½ | TEASPOON DRY MUSTARD |
| 1 | CUP CHOPPED CRYSTALLIZED GINGER (ABOUT 5 OUNCES) |

Heat oil in heavy large Dutch oven over medium-high heat. Add shallots and sauté until beginning to brown, about 8 minutes. Add Marsala and sugar and stir until sugar dissolves. Add cranberries, curry powder and mustard. Bring to boil, reduce heat to medium and boil gently until berries pop, stirring occasionally, about 7 minutes. Remove from heat and mix in ginger. Cool. Season relish with salt. Cover and refrigerate. *(Can be prepared 3 days ahead. Keep refrigerated.)*

## Upscale Macaroni and Cheese

*Everyone's favorite childhood dish gets a sophisticated twist with the addition of red bell peppers, celery and blue cheese.*

**12 servings**

| | |
|---|---|
| 2 | TABLESPOONS (¼ STICK) BUTTER |
| 3 | LARGE RED BELL PEPPERS, CUT INTO ½-INCH PIECES |
| 5 | CELERY STALKS, CHOPPED |
| 1½ | CUPS WHIPPING CREAM |
| 1½ | CUPS HALF AND HALF |
| 1 | POUND BLUE CHEESE, CRUMBLED |
| 1 | TEASPOON CELERY SEEDS |
| | CAYENNE PEPPER |
| 3 | EGG YOLKS |
| ½ | CUP CHOPPED CELERY LEAVES |
| 1 | POUND PENNE |
| ¾ | CUP FRESHLY GRATED PARMESAN CHEESE (ABOUT 2 OUNCES) |

Melt butter in heavy large skillet over medium-high heat. Add bell peppers and celery and sauté until just beginning to soften, about 7 minutes. Remove vegetables from heat. Season with salt and pepper.

Combine cream, half and half and blue cheese in heavy medium saucepan. Stir over low heat until cheese melts. Remove from heat. Add celery seeds. Season sauce with cayenne, salt and pepper. Beat yolks in medium bowl to blend. Gradually whisk in half of cheese sauce. Return mixture to saucepan and whisk to blend. Add chopped celery leaves to sauce.

Butter 13¾ x 10½ x 2¾-inch (4-quart capacity) oval baking dish. Cook pasta in pot of boiling salted water until just tender but still firm to bite, stirring occasionally. Drain. Return to same pot. Add sauce and vegetables; stir to blend. Transfer to baking dish. *(Can be made 1 day ahead. Cover; refrigerate. Let stand 1 hour before continuing.)*

Preheat oven to 400°F. Sprinkle Parmesan over surface of pasta. Bake until pasta is heated through, sauce is bubbling and top is beginning to brown, about 25 minutes.

## Brussels Sprouts Salad with Lemon-Thyme Vinaigrette

*Even people who swear they don't like brussels sprouts will enjoy this pretty and refreshing salad.*

**12 servings**

| | |
|---|---|
| 3 | POUNDS FRESH BRUSSELS SPROUTS, ENDS TRIMMED, HALVED THROUGH STEM |
| ¼ | CUP FRESH LEMON JUICE |
| 1 | TABLESPOON PLUS 1 TEASPOON DIJON MUSTARD |
| 1 | CUP OLIVE OIL |
| 1 | TABLESPOON CHOPPED FRESH THYME OR 1 TEASPOON DRIED |
| 6 | HEADS BELGIAN ENDIVE, CUT INTO 1½-INCH PIECES |
| 1 | LARGE HEAD RADICCHIO, CUT INTO 1½-INCH PIECES |

Cook brussels sprouts in large pot of boiling salted water until just tender, about 8 minutes. Drain. Rinse with cold water and drain well. Transfer to medium bowl. Combine lemon juice and mustard in small bowl. Gradually whisk in oil. Add thyme. Season to taste with salt and pepper. *(Can be prepared 1 day ahead. Cover brussels sprouts and dressing separately and refrigerate. Bring to room temperature before continuing.)*

Combine endive and radicchio on platter or in large shallow bowl. Toss with enough dressing to coat lightly. Mix brussels sprouts with remaining dressing. Mound atop salad and serve.

OPPOSITE: UPSCALE MACARONI AND CHEESE AND CORN BREAD WITH SUN-DRIED TOMATOES.

## Corn Bread with Sun-dried Tomatoes

*Serve any leftovers warm for breakfast or a late-afternoon snack.*

**12 servings**

| | |
|---|---|
| 3 | CUPS YELLOW CORNMEAL |
| 1½ | CUPS ALL PURPOSE FLOUR |
| ½ | CUP SUGAR |
| 1 | TABLESPOON DRIED RUBBED SAGE |
| 1 | TABLESPOON PEPPER |
| 1½ | TEASPOONS SALT |
| 1½ | TEASPOONS BAKING POWDER |
| ¾ | TEASPOON BAKING SODA |
| 2¼ | CUPS BUTTERMILK |
| 1 | CUP CHOPPED DRAINED OIL-PACKED SUN-DRIED TOMATOES, ¼ CUP OIL RESERVED |
| ½ | CUP (1 STICK) BUTTER, MELTED, COOLED |
| 4 | LARGE EGGS |
| 1 | LARGE EGG YOLK |

Preheat oven to 400°F. Butter two 9½-inch-diameter deep-dish pie dishes. Combine cornmeal, flour, sugar, sage, pepper, salt, baking powder and baking soda in large bowl and whisk to blend. Combine buttermilk, sun-dried tomatoes, reserved sun-dried tomato oil, butter, eggs and egg yolk in medium bowl and whisk to blend. Stir buttermilk mixture into dry ingredients. Divide corn bread batter between prepared pie dishes.

Bake corn breads until tops begin to brown and tester inserted into center comes out clean, about 30 minutes. Cool slightly. *(Corn breads can be prepared 6 hours ahead. Cool completely. Cover with aluminum foil. Reheat covered in 350°F oven about 10 minutes.)*

Cut corn breads into wedges. Transfer to towel-lined basket; serve warm.

## Fruitcake Brownies

*These irresistible treats are filled with dried apricots, figs and cherries as well as dates and walnuts, and are topped with a cream cheese frosting. Offer decorated Christmas cookies alongside.*

**makes about 24**

**BROWNIES**

| | |
|---|---|
| 1 | CUP (2 STICKS) UNSALTED BUTTER |
| 9 | OUNCES SEMISWEET CHOCOLATE, CHOPPED |
| 1½ | OUNCES UNSWEETENED CHOCOLATE, CHOPPED |
| 1 | CUP PLUS 2 TABLESPOONS SUGAR |
| 3 | LARGE EGGS |
| 1½ | TEASPOONS VANILLA EXTRACT |
| 1 | CUP ALL PURPOSE FLOUR |
| 1 | TEASPOON BAKING POWDER |
| ¼ | TEASPOON SALT |
| ½ | CUP CHOPPED WALNUTS |
| ⅓ | CUP CHOPPED DRIED APRICOTS |
| ⅓ | CUP CHOPPED DRIED FIGS |
| ⅓ | CUP CHOPPED PITTED DATES |
| ⅓ | CUP DRIED SOUR CHERRIES OR DRIED CURRANTS |

**FROSTING**

| | |
|---|---|
| 1 | 8-OUNCE PACKAGE CREAM CHEESE, ROOM TEMPERATURE |
| ¼ | CUP (½ STICK) UNSALTED BUTTER, ROOM TEMPERATURE |
| 1 | TABLESPOON VANILLA EXTRACT |
| 2 | CUPS SIFTED POWDERED SUGAR |

WALNUT HALVES (OPTIONAL)

FOR BROWNIES: Preheat oven to 350°F. Butter 13 x 9 x 2-inch glass baking dish. Combine 1 cup butter and semisweet and unsweetened chocolates in heavy medium saucepan. Stir over low heat until chocolates melt and mixture is smooth. Cool to lukewarm.

Using electric mixer, beat sugar and 3 eggs in large bowl until very thick and pale, about 3 minutes. Stir in chocolate mixture and vanilla extract. Whisk 1 cup flour, baking powder and salt in medium bowl to blend. Stir dry ingredients into chocolate mixture. Mix in walnuts and dried fruits.

Transfer batter to prepared dish; smooth top. Bake until top cracks and tester inserted into center comes out with a few moist crumbs attached, about 35 minutes. Cool in pan on rack.

FOR FROSTING: Combine room temperature cream cheese, butter and vanilla extract in processor. Blend until smooth, scraping down sides of bowl occasionally. Add sugar and process to blend. Spread frosting over brownies. Refrigerate until frosting is well chilled, about 2 hours. *(Can be prepared 3 days ahead. Cover; keep refrigerated.)*

Cut brownies into squares. Arrange on platter; garnish with walnuts.

OPPOSITE: BRUSSELS SPROUTS SALAD WITH LEMON-THYME VINAIGRETTE AND HONEY-GLAZED HAM WITH CRANBERRY-SHALLOT RELISH.

## BREAKFAST *with* SAINT NICK *for* EIGHT

BRANDY MILK PUNCH

SCRAMBLED EGGS *with* CHIVES, SMOKED TROUT *and* TOMATOES

CARAMELIZED BACON

CINNAMON POPPY SEED CAKE

FRESH JUICES

COFFEE

## Brandy Milk Punch

**8 servings**

2½  CUPS VERY COLD MILK
1  CUP BRANDY
½  CUP COFFEE LIQUEUR
2  TABLESPOONS VANILLA EXTRACT
½  TEASPOON (SCANT) GROUND NUTMEG
10  ICE CUBES

Place half of each ingredient in blender. Blend on high until punch is smooth and frothy. Pour punch into 4 glasses. Repeat process with remaining ingredients and serve.

## Scrambled Eggs with Chives, Smoked Trout and Tomatoes

**8 servings**

4  TOMATOES, HALVED

12  LARGE EGGS
⅓  CUP HALF AND HALF
¼  CUP (½ STICK) BUTTER
2  TABLESPOONS CHOPPED FRESH CHIVES OR GREEN ONIONS

1  POUND SMOKED TROUT, SKINNED, BONED, FLAKED OR 6 OUNCES SMOKED SALMON, CUT INTO SMALL PIECES

Position rack about 6 inches from broiler and preheat. Arrange tomatoes cut side up on baking sheet. Broil until lightly colored and tender, watching closely to avoid burning, about 5 minutes. Remove from broiler. Season tomatoes to taste with salt and pepper. Tent with foil to keep warm.

Whisk eggs and half and half in large bowl. Season with salt and pepper. Melt butter in heavy large nonstick skillet over low heat. Add egg mixture and cook until almost set, stirring frequently, about 6 minutes. Stir in chopped chives. Remove from heat.

Spoon eggs into center of large platter. Sprinkle with smoked trout. Arrange tomatoes around edge of platter and serve immediately.

## Caramelized Bacon

**8 servings**

1½  CUPS FIRMLY PACKED GOLDEN BROWN SUGAR
1  POUND BACON (DO NOT USE THICK-SLICED)

Preheat oven to 350°F. Place sugar in shallow pan. Add strips of bacon to pan and turn to coat completely with sugar. Transfer to large broiler pan or rack set over baking sheet with rim.

Bake bacon until dark golden brown, turning once, about 8 minutes per side. Using tongs, transfer to rack and cool. *(Can be prepared 2 hours ahead. Store in airtight container at room temperature.)* Serve at room temperature.

## Cinnamon Poppy Seed Cake

**8 to 10 servings**

2  CUPS SUGAR
1  TABLESPOON GROUND CINNAMON
2½  CUPS ALL PURPOSE FLOUR
2  TEASPOONS BAKING POWDER
1  TEASPOON BAKING SODA
½  TEASPOON SALT

1  CUP (2 STICKS) UNSALTED BUTTER, ROOM TEMPERATURE
2  TEASPOONS VANILLA EXTRACT
4  LARGE EGGS, SEPARATED
1  CUP BUTTERMILK
6  TABLESPOONS POPPY SEEDS

Preheat oven to 350°F. Generously butter 12-cup Bundt pan. Combine ½ cup sugar and cinnamon in small bowl. Sift flour, baking powder, baking soda and salt into medium bowl.

Using electric mixer, beat butter and vanilla in large bowl until fluffy. Gradually add 1 cup sugar, beating until mixture is smooth. Beat in egg yolks 1 at a time. Mix in flour mixture alternately with buttermilk in 3 additions each. Fold in poppy seeds. Using clean dry beaters, beat whites in medium bowl until soft peaks form. Gradually add remaining ½ cup sugar, beating until stiff but not dry. Fold whites into batter in 2 additions.

Spoon half of batter into prepared pan. Sprinkle with half of cinnamon sugar. Spoon remaining batter over. Sprinkle with remaining cinnamon sugar.

Bake cake until tester inserted near center comes out clean, about 50 minutes. Cool cake in pan on rack 10 minutes. Turn cake out onto rack and cool completely. *(Can be prepared 1 day ahead. Wrap in foil and let stand at room temperature.)* Cut cake into wedges.

OPPOSITE: SCRAMBLED EGGS WITH CHIVES, SMOKED TROUT AND TOMATOES AND CARAMELIZED BACON.

# CHRISTMAS DINNER *for* TEN

PÂTÉ *with* TOASTED BRIOCHE

CHAMPAGNE

ROAST PRIME RIB *of* BEEF *with*
HERBED YORKSHIRE PUDDINGS

DEVILED CAULIFLOWER

BUTTERED PEAS *with*
PEARL ONIONS

WATERCRESS SALAD

RED BORDEAUX

CHRISTMAS PUDDING *with*
GINGERED RUM HARD SAUCE

STILTON *and* WALNUTS

PORT

## Roast Prime Rib of Beef with Herbed Yorkshire Puddings

*Prime rib is, and always has been, among the grandest holiday main courses. Here it is presented simply, accompanied by individual, herb-flecked Yorkshire puddings, the quintessential partner for roast beef. To go with the entrée, serve buttered peas and pearl onions and a watercress salad, and pour a red Bordeaux throughout the meal.*

**10 servings**

YORKSHIRE PUDDINGS

- 2 CUPS ALL PURPOSE FLOUR
- 1 TEASPOON SALT
- 1 CUP MILK
- 1 CUP WATER
- 4 LARGE EGGS
- 3 TABLESPOONS MINCED FRESH CHIVES OR GREEN ONIONS
- 2 TABLESPOONS MINCED FRESH TARRAGON OR 2 TEASPOONS DRIED
- ½ TEASPOON PEPPER

BEEF

- 1 10-POUND BEEF RIB ROAST FROM SMALL END (ABOUT 5 RIBS)

PREPARED WHITE HORSERADISH

FOR YORKSHIRE PUDDINGS: Combine flour and salt in medium bowl. Combine milk and water in large glass measuring cup. Gradually add milk mixture to flour, beating until smooth. Add eggs, 1 at a time, beating well after each addition. Stir in herbs and pepper. Cover and refrigerate at least 1 hour. *(Batter can be made 8 hours ahead. Keep refrigerated. Rewhisk before using.)*

FOR BEEF: Position rack in center of oven and preheat to 325°F. Arrange roast fat side up in shallow roasting pan. Season with salt and pepper. Roast until meat thermometer inserted into thickest part of roast registers 120°F for rare, occasionally spooning off and reserving fat from pan, about 2 hours 50 minutes. Remove from oven; tent roast with foil.

Increase oven temperature to 450°F. Measure 1 tablespoon reserved beef fat into each of ten 1⅓-cup glass custard dishes. Place dishes on baking sheet. Place sheet with dishes in oven and heat just until fat begins to smoke, about 8 minutes. Remove sheet from oven. Divide batter equally among dishes, allotting about generous ⅓ cup per dish. Bake puddings 15 minutes. Reduce oven temperature to 350°F and bake until edges of puddings are golden and center is puffed , about 25 minutes (puddings will sink when removed from oven).

Carve roast and serve with puddings, passing horseradish separately.

## Deviled Cauliflower

*Deviled is an old-fashioned term for "highly seasoned," and this dish is enhanced by a white sauce flavored with mustard and Worcestershire.*

**10 servings**

- 2 MEDIUM HEADS CAULIFLOWER, TRIMMED, CUT INTO FLORETS
- 3 TABLESPOONS BUTTER
- 3 TABLESPOONS ALL PURPOSE FLOUR
- 1¾ CUPS MILK
- 1 BAY LEAF
  PINCH OF GROUND NUTMEG
- 2 TABLESPOONS DIJON MUSTARD
- 1 TEASPOON WORCESTERSHIRE SAUCE
- ½ CUP FRESH WHITE BREADCRUMBS
- 2 TABLESPOONS BUTTER, MELTED

Cook cauliflower in pot of boiling water until crisp-tender, about 5 minutes. Drain. Rinse under cold water. Drain thoroughly.

Melt 3 tablespoons butter in heavy small saucepan over low heat. Add flour and stir 5 minutes. Gradually whisk in milk. Add bay leaf and nutmeg and bring to simmer, stirring often. Cover partially; cook until thick, stirring often, about 5 minutes. Stir in mustard and Worcestershire. Season sauce with salt and pepper. Discard bay leaf. Transfer sauce to large bowl. Add cauliflower to sauce and stir until well coated. *(Can be prepared 1 day ahead. Cover and refrigerate.)*

Preheat oven to 350°F. Place cauliflower mixture in 13 x 9 x 2-inch broiler-proof baking dish. Sprinkle breadcrumbs over. Drizzle with butter. Bake until cauliflower is heated through and sauce bubbles at edges, approximately 45 minutes.

Preheat broiler. Place dish under broiler; cook until breadcrumbs are golden, 2 minutes. Cool 5 minutes.

OPPOSITE: ROAST PRIME RIB OF BEEF WITH HERBED YORKSHIRE PUDDINGS.

## Christmas Pudding with Gingered Rum Hard Sauce

*This dessert is an excellent solution for today's busy cooks, because it can be prepared up to two months ahead. It also makes a lovely gift when wrapped in cellophane and tied with a bow. For a beautiful presentation at the table, heat a small amount of dark rum in a heavy small skillet until just warm. Carefully ignite the rum with a long match and pour the flaming liquor over the pudding. For a sophisticated finale, follow the pudding with Stilton cheese, walnuts and Port.*

**10 to 12 servings**

| | |
|---|---|
| 1 | CUP ALL PURPOSE FLOUR |
| ¾ | TEASPOON BAKING POWDER |
| ½ | TEASPOON SALT |
| ½ | TEASPOON GROUND NUTMEG |
| ½ | TEASPOON GROUND ALLSPICE |
| ½ | TEASPOON GROUND GINGER |
| ¼ | TEASPOON GROUND CINNAMON |
| 1 | CUP DRIED TART CHERRIES |
| 1 | CUP CHOPPED DRIED APRICOTS |
| 1 | CUP CHOPPED PITTED DATES |
| 1 | CUP GOLDEN RAISINS |
| ¾ | CUP DRIED CURRANTS |
| 3½ | CUPS FRESH WHITE BREADCRUMBS |
| ¼ | CUP MINCED CRYSTALLIZED GINGER |
| 6 | OUNCES CHILLED BEEF SUET* |
| 1 | CUP FIRMLY PACKED DARK BROWN SUGAR |
| ½ | CUP APPLE BUTTER |
| ⅓ | CUP DARK RUM |
| 3 | LARGE EGGS |
| 1 | TEASPOON VANILLA EXTRACT |
| ¼ | TEASPOON ALMOND EXTRACT |

GINGERED RUM HARD SAUCE
(SEE RECIPE AT RIGHT)

Generously butter 2½-quart pudding mold or thick heatproof glass bowl. Sift first 7 ingredients into large bowl. Add cherries, apricots, dates, raisins and currants and toss to coat with flour. Stir in breadcrumbs with ginger. Finely chop suet in food processor. Add to breadcumb mixture and toss to coat. Stir in sugar. Whisk apple butter, rum, eggs and extracts in medium bowl. Add to breadcrumb mixture and stir until batter is well combined (batter will be thick).

Spoon batter into prepared mold. Smooth top with spatula. Cover mold tightly with heavy-duty foil. Place rack in large pot. Set pudding on rack. Pour enough water into pot to come halfway up sides of mold. Cover pot. Bring water to simmer over medium-low heat. Steam pudding until cooked through, adding more boiling water to pot as necessary, about 5 hours. Transfer mold to rack and cool 30 minutes. Turn out pudding. *(Can be made up to 2 months ahead. Cool completely. Wrap tightly in plastic and refrigerate. To reheat pudding, unwrap and return to buttered mold. Place mold on rack in large pot. Pour enough hot water into pot to come halfway up sides of mold. Cover pot; steam pudding over medium-low heat until heated through, about 2½ hours. Transfer to rack. Let stand 30 minutes. Turn out pudding.)* Transfer warm pudding to platter. Serve with Gingered Rum Hard Sauce.

*\*Available at butcher shops and also at some specialty foods stores.*

## Gingered Rum Hard Sauce

**makes about 2 cups**

| | |
|---|---|
| 1 | CUP (2 STICKS) UNSALTED BUTTER, ROOM TEMPERATURE |
| 1 | CUP POWDERED SUGAR |
| ¼ | CUP DARK RUM |
| ⅓ | CUP MINCED CRYSTALLIZED GINGER |

Using electric mixer, beat butter in medium bowl until creamy. Add sugar and beat until well blended. Beat in rum. Stir in ginger. *(Can be prepared 3 days ahead. Cover and refrigerate. Bring to room temperature before serving.)*

OPPOSITE: CHRISTMAS PUDDING WITH GINGERED RUM HARD SAUCE.

FRUITCAKE, RUM BALLS AND MINCEMEAT ARE ALL WELL AND GOOD, BUT CHRISTMAS WOULDN'T BE CHRISTMAS WITHOUT DECORATED COOKIES. HERE, WE OFFER TWO EASY-TO-MAKE COOKIE RECIPES—CITRUS SUGAR COOKIES AND GINGERBREAD COOKIES—PLUS STEP-BY-STEP INSTRUCTIONS FOR GLAZING, PIPING AND DRIZZLING. EVEN OLD SAINT NICK WILL BE IMPRESSED WITH THE COOKIE THAT ACCOMPANIES HIS GLASS OF MILK.

## *Gingerbread Cookies and Citrus Sugar Cookies*

*Each recipe makes about three dozen cookies, depending on the size of the cookie cutters used. The gingerbread cookies are crisp and lightly spiced, while the sugar cookies have lively lemon and tangerine flavors. Both are perfect for a variety of imaginative decorations.*

### GINGERBREAD COOKIE DOUGH

- 2¾ CUPS UNBLEACHED ALL PURPOSE FLOUR
- 1 TEASPOON GROUND GINGER
- ¾ TEASPOON BAKING SODA
- ½ TEASPOON GROUND CINNAMON
- ½ TEASPOON GROUND CLOVES
- ¼ CUP SOLID VEGETABLE SHORTENING, ROOM TEMPERATURE
- ¼ CUP (½ STICK) UNSALTED BUTTER, ROOM TEMPERATURE
- ½ CUP SUGAR
- ½ CUP UNSULFURED (LIGHT) MOLASSES
- 1 LARGE EGG

### CITRUS SUGAR COOKIE DOUGH

- 2 CUPS UNBLEACHED ALL PURPOSE FLOUR
- 1½ TEASPOONS BAKING POWDER
- ¼ TEASPOON SALT
- ¾ CUP (1½ STICKS) UNSALTED BUTTER, ROOM TEMPERATURE
- 1¼ TEASPOONS GRATED LEMON PEEL
- 1¼ TEASPOONS GRATED TANGERINE PEEL OR ORANGE PEEL

- ½ CUP SUGAR
- ¼ CUP POWDERED SUGAR
- 1 LARGE EGG

### POWDERED SUGAR ICING

- 6 TABLESPOONS FRESH LEMON JUICE
- ¼ CUP MILK
- 6 TO 8 CUPS POWDERED SUGAR

ASSORTED FOOD COLORINGS (SUCH AS BLUE, RED, YELLOW AND GREEN)

### DECORATING COOKIES

MILK

PASTRY BRUSHES

ASSORTED DECORATIONS (SUCH AS COLORED SUGAR, SWEETENED SHREDDED COCONUT, TOASTED SLICED ALMONDS, CHOCOLATE AND RAINBOW SPRINKLES, MULTI-COLORED NONPAREILS, BUTTON CANDIES, MINI SEMISWEET BAKING BITS AND DRIED CURRANTS)

STANDARD PASTRY BAGS AND 1/16-INCH PLAIN TIPS OR DISPOSABLE PLASTIC PASTRY BAGS*

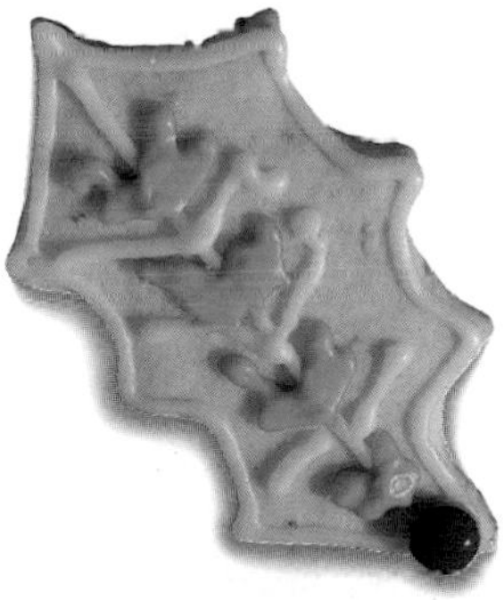

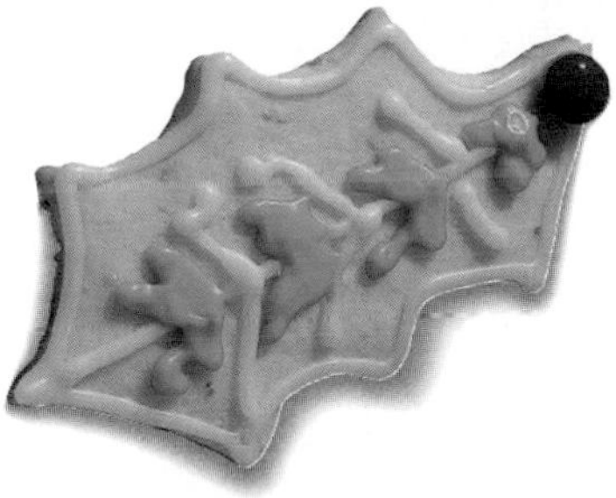

**FOR GINGERBREAD COOKIE DOUGH:** Sift flour, ginger, baking soda, cinnamon and cloves into medium bowl. Using electric mixer, beat shortening and butter in large bowl until light. Add sugar and beat until fluffy. Beat in molasses, then egg. Add dry ingredients. Using spoon, stir until mixture forms dough (dough will be very soft). Divide dough into thirds. Gather each third into ball; flatten into disks. Wrap each disk in plastic and refrigerate until firm, about 4 hours. *(Can be prepared 2 days ahead. Keep refrigerated.)*

**FOR CITRUS SUGAR COOKIE DOUGH:** Sift flour, baking powder and salt into medium bowl. Using electric mixer, beat butter, lemon peel and tangerine peel in large bowl until light. Add ½ cup sugar and ¼ cup powdered sugar and beat until fluffy. Beat in egg. Add dry ingredients. Using spoon, stir until mixture forms dough (dough will be soft). Divide dough into thirds. Gather each third into ball; flatten into disks. Wrap each disk in plastic and refrigerate until firm, about 4 hours. *(Can be prepared 2 days ahead. Keep refrigerated. Let dough soften slightly, if necessary, before rolling out.)*

Preheat oven to 350°F. Generously flour work surface and rolling pin. Place 1 dough disk on work surface (keep remaining 2 dough disks refrigerated; work with one type of dough at a time.). Press rolling pin into dough several times to flatten slightly for easier rolling. Roll out dough to ⅛- to ¼-inch thickness, frequently lifting and turning dough to prevent sticking. Using assorted cookie cutters dipped into flour, cut out cookies. Transfer cookies to ungreased nonstick baking sheets, spacing ½ inch apart. Gather scraps together and reserve.

Bake until cookies turn brown on edges, about 15 minutes. Let cookies stand on sheets 1 minute. Using metal spatula, transfer cookies to racks and cool completely. Repeat rolling, cutting and baking with remaining 2 dough disks as described above, being sure to cool cookie sheets before making each batch. Combine all reserved dough scraps and shape into ball; flatten into disk. Wrap disk in plastic and freeze until firm enough to roll, about 30 minutes. Repeat rolling, cutting and baking as described above. Store airtight at room temperature.

**FOR ICING:** Combine lemon juice and milk in large bowl. Whisk in 5 cups powdered sugar. Gradually whisk in enough remaining sugar by ½ cupfuls to form icing stiff enough to pipe (mixture will resemble stirred sour cream). Transfer ⅔ cup icing to small bowl to use as white icing; set aside. Divide remaining icing equally among 2 or more small bowls; mix food coloring by drops into each bowl, tinting icing to desired shade. If necessary, stir more sugar into icing to thicken.

## Decorating Cookies

**TO GLAZE:** Spoon a small amount of white or colored icing into small bowl. Mix in enough milk by ¼ teaspoonfuls to thin icing to spreading consistency. Using pastry brush, brush glaze over cooled baked cookies. Continue decorating glazed cookies, if desired, using the following techniques.

**TO SPRINKLE WITH DECORATIONS:** Before glaze dries, sprinkle cookies with assorted decorations.

**TO PIPE USING STANDARD PASTRY BAGS:** Fit each pastry bag with 1/16-inch plain tip. Stand each bag in short cup. Fold back top of bag to expose interior. Spoon 1 color of icing into each bag. Lift bag from cup; twist top of bag at level of icing to close securely.

**TO PIPE USING DISPOSABLE PLASTIC PASTRY BAGS:** Stand each plastic bag in short cup. Spoon 1 color of icing into each bag. Lift bag from cup; twist tip of bag at level of icing to close securely. Cut off very bottom of tip to allow small ribbon of icing to come out.

Pipe icing decoratively onto plain or glazed cookies. Before piped icing sets, sprinkle with colored sugar, coconut or other decorations, if desired.

**TO DRIZZLE:** Line baking sheets with foil. Place plain or glazed cookies on foil, spacing apart. Mix milk into white or colored icing by ½ teaspoonfuls until icing is thin enough to drizzle. Dip spoon into icing and drizzle over cookies in zigzag or slanted lines. Before icing lines set, sprinkle with colored sugar, sweetened shredded coconut or other decorations, if desired.

**TO APPLY DECORATIONS:** Use wet icing as glue to stick on nuts, dried currants or other decorations 1 at a time. For example, dip tip of toasted sliced almond into icing. Attach iced section of almond to plain or glazed cookie. Repeat to form 1 row of nuts or to cover cookie completely.

Let decorated cookies stand until icing sets, about 2 hours. *(Can be prepared up to 2 weeks ahead. Store cookies in single layers between sheets of waxed paper in airtight containers.)*

*\*Available at some cookware stores or cake and candy supply stores.*

1. SET UP AND READY TO GO: COOKIE CUTTERS; FOOD COLORING; NONPAREILS; COLORED SUGAR; SPRINKLES; PASTRY BRUSHES, PASTRY BAGS AND TIPS; SLICED ALMONDS; MINI SEMISWEET BAKING BITS; AND COCONUT.

2. TO MAKE THE CHILLED SUGAR COOKIE DOUGH EASIER TO ROLL, BEGIN BY FIRMLY PRESSING A GENEROUSLY FLOURED ROLLING PIN INTO THE CHILLED DOUGH DISK SEVERAL TIMES TO FLATTEN SLIGHTLY.

3. BEFORE USING THE COOKIE CUTTERS, BE SURE TO DIP THEM INTO FLOUR TO PREVENT THE DOUGH FROM STICKING.

4. FOR ICING STIFF ENOUGH TO PIPE ONTO COOKIES, GRADUALLY WHISK IN POWDERED SUGAR BY 1/2 CUPFULS UNTIL MIXTURE RESEMBLES STIRRED SOUR CREAM.

5. TO PREPARE THE GLAZE, THIN SOME OF THE ICING TO SPREADING CONSISTENCY WITH ADDITIONAL MILK. USE A PASTRY BRUSH TO COAT THE COOKIES.

6. FILLING A PASTRY BAG IS EASY. STAND THE BAG (FITTED WITH A TIP) IN A CUP. FOLD BACK THE TOP OF THE BAG TO EXPOSE INTERIOR. SPOON ICING INTO THE BAG. LIFT BAG; TWIST AT TOP LEVEL OF ICING TO CLOSE.

7. AN ALTERNATIVE TO THE STANDARD PASTRY BAG IS A DISPOSABLE PLASTIC BAG. AFTER FILLING THE PLASTIC BAG WITH ICING, USE SCISSORS TO CUT OFF THE VERY BOTTOM OF THE TIP, ALLOWING THE ICING TO COME OUT.

8. THE COOKIES CAN BE DECORATED IN A VARIETY OF WAYS. SIMPLY SQUEEZE THE BAG TO RELEASE THE ICING, AND PIPE DOTS, LINES OR OTHER DESIGNS ONTO THE COOKIES.

9. FOR AN EVEN EASIER DESIGN TECHNIQUE (NO PASTRY BAG NECESSARY), DRIZZLE THE ICING OFF A SPOON TO CREATE A PRETTY ZIGZAG EFFECT.

# MORE GIFTS *from the* KITCHEN

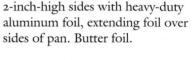

Of all the sweets you give during the holidays, homemade goodies are the best: They taste delicious, are always appreciated, and don't involve spending hours in a crowded mall.

Here are five luscious treats to share with everyone on your list, including candies, cakes and cookies—all with ideas for gift wrapping, too. Just be sure to prepare extra, to give your own Christmas spirit a boost.

## Hazelnut Caramels

*Wrapped in colorful cellophane, these chewy caramels (below) make a great gift for friends with a sweet tooth. And since the candies can be made two weeks ahead, their preparation won't interfere with all the activity around December 25.*

### makes 81 pieces

| | |
|---|---|
| 1 | CUP (2 STICKS) UNSALTED BUTTER |
| 1¼ | CUPS FIRMLY PACKED GOLDEN BROWN SUGAR |
| 1 | CUP SUGAR |
| 1¼ | CUPS DARK CORN SYRUP |
| 1 | 14-OUNCE CAN SWEETENED CONDENSED MILK |
| 1 | VANILLA BEAN, SPLIT LENGTHWISE |
| 1 | CUP COARSELY CHOPPED HUSKED TOASTED HAZELNUTS (ABOUT 4 OUNCES) |
| | CELLOPHANE |

Line 9-inch square baking pan with 2-inch-high sides with heavy-duty aluminum foil, extending foil over sides of pan. Butter foil.

Melt 1 cup butter in heavy large saucepan over low heat. Add both sugars, corn syrup and sweetened condensed milk and stir until sugar dissolves. Scrape seeds from vanilla bean into mixture; add bean. Attach clip-on candy thermometer to side of saucepan. Increase heat to medium and bring mixture to boil. Cook mixture 8 minutes, stirring frequently.

Using tongs, remove vanilla bean and discard. Continue cooking until candy thermometer registers 242°F, stirring frequently, about 5 minutes longer. Immediately remove from heat; stir in hazelnuts. Quickly pour caramel into prepared pan (do not scrape saucepan). Cool until almost firm, about 1 hour.

Using buttered heavy large knife, score 8 lines lengthwise to depth of ¼ inch in caramel, then score 8 lines crosswise. Using aluminum foil as aid, lift caramel out of pan. Using same buttered heavy large knife, cut caramel on scored lines into pieces. Wrap each piece of caramel in cellophane. *(Can be prepared 2 weeks ahead. Store caramels in airtight container.)*

## Individual Orange and Poppy Seed Pound Cakes

*These little cakes (right) can be put in the center of a gift basket filled with other goodies, or wrapped in foil and festive holiday paper to be given on their own.*

### makes 4 cakes

| | |
|---|---|
| 2 | CUPS ALL PURPOSE FLOUR |
| 1 | TEASPOON BAKING POWDER |
| ½ | TEASPOON SALT |
| 1¾ | CUPS SUGAR |
| 1¼ | CUPS (2½ STICKS) UNSALTED BUTTER, ROOM TEMPERATURE |
| 5 | LARGE EGGS |
| ⅓ | CUP ORANGE JUICE |
| 1 | TABLESPOON GRATED ORANGE PEEL |
| 1 | TEASPOON VANILLA EXTRACT |
| ¼ | CUP POPPY SEEDS |

Preheat oven to 350°F. Butter and flour four 5⅜ x 3¼ x 1⅞-inch loaf pans. Sift flour, baking powder and salt into medium bowl. Using electric mixer, beat sugar and unsalted butter in large bowl until light and fluffy. Add eggs 1 at a time, beating well after each addition. Beat in orange juice, grated orange peel and vanilla extract (batter may look curdled). Beat in flour mixture. Fold in poppy seeds.

Divide batter equally among prepared pans (about 1½ cups each). Place pans in oven. Bake until tops of cakes are brown and tester inserted into center comes out clean, about 55 minutes. Transfer pans to racks. Cool cakes for 10 minutes. Cut around sides of pans to loosen cakes. Turn cakes out onto wire racks and cool completely. *(Cakes can be prepared up to 1 week ahead. Wrap in foil; store cakes at room temperature.)*

## Puff Pastry Pinwheel Cookies with Jam

*Supermarket staples—puff pastry and fruit jams—are transformed into delicate teatime treats (below) that require very little effort. For gift giving, place the cookies between sheets of waxed paper or tissue paper, and pack them in a pretty tin. Or if you want to take them to a party for same-day eating, arrange them in a decorative bag filled with tissue.*

### makes 40

| | |
|---|---|
| 1 | 17¼-OUNCE PACKAGE FROZEN PUFF PASTRY (2 SHEETS), THAWED |
| 1 | EGG, BEATEN TO BLEND (GLAZE) |
| ½ | CUP (ABOUT) SUGAR |
| ½ | CUP (ABOUT) ASSORTED JAMS (SUCH AS RASPBERRY, APRICOT AND KIWI) |
| | POWDERED SUGAR (OPTIONAL) |

Preheat oven to 400°F. Lightly butter 2 heavy large baking sheets. Roll out 1 puff pastry sheet on lightly floured surface to 16 x 13-inch rectangle. Trim edges neatly, forming 15 x 12-inch rectangle. Cut rectangle into twenty 3-inch squares. Using small sharp knife, make 1-inch-long diagonal cut in all 4 corners of 1 square, cutting toward center (do not cut through center). To form pinwheels, fold every other point of puff pastry toward center of square, pressing to adhere. Repeat with remaining puff pastry squares.

Brush pinwheels lightly with egg glaze. Sprinkle each with ½ teaspoon sugar. Place scant ½ teaspoon jam in center of each. Transfer to prepared baking sheet. Bake until pinwheels are golden and puffed, about 13 minutes. Using metal spatula, transfer cookies to rack and cool. Repeat with remaining puff pastry sheet, glaze, sugar and jam.

Sprinkle cookies with powdered sugar, if desired. *(Can be prepared ahead. Place cookies between waxed paper sheets in airtight containers and freeze up to 2 weeks, thaw before packing, or store airtight at room temperature up to 3 days.)*

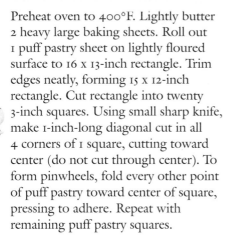

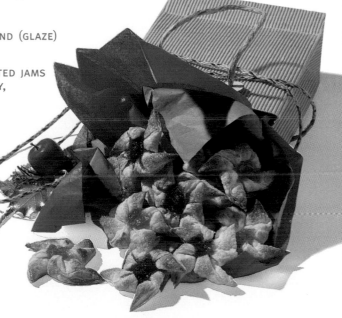

## Caramel-Almond Popcorn

*This crunchy old-time favorite (below) is an ideal gift for families, because both adults and children will eat it by the handful. For a gift, place the popcorn in glass jars tied with ribbon and decorated with sprigs of holly. And for immediate eating, put the popcorn in a cellophane-lined basket, and set it out for all to enjoy.*

**makes 10 cups**

½  CUP POPCORN KERNELS, FRESHLY POPPED

2  CUPS WHOLE ALMONDS

1¼  CUPS FIRMLY PACKED GOLDEN BROWN SUGAR

¼  CUP (½ STICK) UNSALTED BUTTER

¼  CUP LIGHT CORN SYRUP

2  TEASPOONS VANILLA EXTRACT

½  TEASPOON ALMOND EXTRACT

½  TEASPOON SALT

¼  TEASPOON BAKING SODA

Preheat oven to 250°F. Generously butter heavy large baking pan. Mix warm popcorn and almonds in prepared pan. Place in oven while preparing syrup.

Combine brown sugar, butter and corn syrup in heavy medium saucepan. Whisk over medium-low heat until sugar dissolves and butter melts. Attach clip-on candy thermometer to side of pan. Increase heat to high and boil without stirring until thermometer registers 255°F, occasionally brushing down sides of pan with wet pastry brush, about 4 minutes. Remove from heat. Stir in vanilla extract, almond extract, salt and baking soda (mixture will bubble). Gradually pour syrup over popcorn and almonds, gently stirring to coat completely.

Bake until caramel feels dry, stirring frequently, about 1 hour 20 minutes. Remove from oven. Using metal spatula, scrape mixture from bottom of pan to loosen. Cool completely in pan. *(Can be prepared 1 week ahead. Store in airtight container at room temperature.)*

## Chocolate-Orange Fruitcake with Pecans

*The perennial Christmas gift gets a luscious face-lift in this impressive cake (opposite). Store the cake in the refrigerator for up to three weeks before giving. Wrap it in some red or green cellophane, and present it in a decorative box (a hatbox is fun) tied with a big bow.*

**16 servings**

CAKE

2½  CUPS LARGE PECAN PIECES, TOASTED

1  CUP (PACKED) CHOPPED DRIED BLACK MISSION FIGS

1  CUP (PACKED) CHOPPED PITTED PRUNES

1  CUP (PACKED) CHOPPED PITTED DATES

½  CUP FROZEN ORANGE JUICE CONCENTRATE, THAWED

¼  CUP GRAND MARNIER OR OTHER ORANGE LIQUEUR

2  TABLESPOONS GRATED ORANGE PEEL

3  CUPS ALL PURPOSE FLOUR

¾  CUP (PACKED) UNSWEETENED COCOA POWDER

2½  TEASPOONS GROUND CINNAMON

1½  TEASPOONS BAKING POWDER

1½  TEASPOONS BAKING SODA

1  TEASPOON SALT

1  1-POUND BOX DARK BROWN SUGAR

6  OUNCES BITTERSWEET (NOT UNSWEETENED) OR SEMISWEET CHOCOLATE, COARSELY CHOPPED

½ cup (1 stick) unsalted butter, room temperature

4 ounces cream cheese, room temperature

4 large eggs, room temperature

¾ cup purchased prune butter*

GLAZE

½ cup plus 2 tablespoons (1¼ sticks) unsalted butter

1 pound bittersweet (not unsweetened) or semisweet chocolate, chopped

6 tablespoons orange juice concentrate, thawed

Chopped candied fruit peel (optional)

FOR CAKE: Position rack in bottom third of oven and preheat to 325°F. Generously butter and flour 12-cup angel food cake pan. Combine toasted pecans, chopped dried figs, prunes, dates, orange juice concentrate, Grand Marnier and grated orange peel in large bowl. Let stand 30 minutes, stirring occasionally.

Sift flour, cocoa, cinnamon, baking powder, baking soda and salt into medium bowl. Combine brown sugar and 6 ounces chocolate in processor and chop into small pieces.

Using electric mixer, beat butter and cream cheese in large bowl to blend. Add chocolate mixture and beat until fluffy. Beat in eggs 1 at a time. Beat in prune butter. Stir in ¼ of dry ingredients. Mix in fruit mixture and remaining dry ingredients in 3 additions each.

Transfer batter to prepared pan. Bake cake until tester inserted near center comes out with a few moist crumbs attached, about 1 hour 55 minutes. Cool 5 minutes. Turn pan over onto rack; let stand 5 minutes. Lift off pan; cool cake completely. Wrap cake in plastic and then store at room temperature for 2 days.

FOR GLAZE: Melt butter in heavy medium saucepan over low heat. Add chopped chocolate; stir until melted and smooth. Whisk in thawed orange juice concentrate.

Place cake on rack. Spread some of chocolate glaze thickly over top and sides of cake. Refrigerate 15 minutes. Spread remaining chocolate glaze over cake, covering completely. Sprinkle with chopped candied fruit peel, if desired. Refrigerate cake at least 30 minutes to set glaze. *(Fruitcake can be prepared up to 3 weeks ahead. Wrap cake in plastic and refrigerate.)*

*Prune butter is available in the kosher section of many supermarkets.*

# NEW YEAR'S EVE

Year's end is a mystical time, loaded with significance. Pegged to the very rotation of the planet around the sun, New Year's can hardly be dismissed as just another excuse to party. As the solar system turns on its silent gears, some sort of celebration seems inevitable and human. If it has been a very good year, we naturally want to send it off in style; if not so good, we also dance and laugh to forget the old and mightily hope for better in the new. New Year's can be spent in a solitary and contemplative way, but most of the time, counting down to the start of the 365 unknown days ahead, we prefer to take strength in numbers.

If that number is two, we recommend a subdued and elegant dinner of pasta, Champagne and chocolate cake, far from the maddening crowds. If crowds are just what you're craving, invite a modest one and whip up this lively appetizer party. Either way, both menus allow you to be on the dance floor, not in the kitchen, as midnight strikes and another year of great parties begins.

# New Year's Eve Appetizer Party *for a* Crowd

Marmalade-glazed
Chicken Wings

Tomato Croutons
*with* Bacon *and* Basil

Toasted Mini Bagels *with*
Smoked Salmon *and* Caviar

Pickled Shrimp

Herbed Phyllo Purses *with*
Camembert *and* Walnuts

Avocado Pâté *with* Parsley
*and* Pistachios

Champagne

## Marmalade-glazed Chicken Wings

*Citrus marmalade adds a zesty sweet and sour taste to these succulent chicken wings. Begin marinating a day ahead. The chicken can be baked a couple of hours before your guests arrive and then quickly reheated. To "flatten" garlic, hit individual cloves with the flat side of a knife.*

**8 to 10 servings**

3  POUNDS CHICKEN WINGS,
   SEPARATED AT JOINTS,
   WING TIPS DISCARDED

½  CUP TEQUILA

½  CUP CHOPPED FRESH CILANTRO

7  TABLESPOONS LIME OR
   LEMON MARMALADE

¼  CUP OLIVE OIL

4  TABLESPOONS FRESH LIME JUICE

1  TABLESPOON COARSELY
   GROUND PEPPER

3  MEDIUM GARLIC CLOVES,
   FLATTENED

1  TEASPOON HOT PEPPER SAUCE
   (SUCH AS TABASCO)

1  TEASPOON SALT

1  TEASPOON GRATED LIME PEEL

2  LIMES, CUT INTO WEDGES
   FRESH CILANTRO SPRIGS

Place chicken wings in large shallow glass baking dish. Mix tequila, chopped cilantro, 3 tablespoons marmalade, oil, 2 tablespoons lime juice, pepper, garlic, hot pepper sauce, salt and ½ teaspoon lime peel in small bowl. Pour over chicken wings. Cover and refrigerate overnight, turning chicken several times.

Preheat oven to 350°F. Remove chicken from marinade and arrange in large shallow baking pan; reserve marinade. Bake chicken 30 minutes, turning pieces occasionally.

Strain marinade into heavy medium saucepan. Boil until reduced by half, stirring occasionally, about 5 minutes. Add remaining 4 tablespoons marmalade, 2 tablespoons lime juice and ½ teaspoon lime peel and boil 1 minute. Brush marinade over chicken.

Preheat broiler. Broil chicken 6 inches from heat source until crisp and brown, turning several times. *(Can be prepared 2 hours ahead. Cover with foil. Uncover and rewarm in 300°F oven before continuing.)* Transfer chicken to platter. Garnish with lime wedges and cilantro sprigs and serve.

## Tomato Croutons with Bacon and Basil

*Two perennial favorites—tomato and basil—are featured in this light, fresh-tasting hors d'oeuvre. Both the croutons and the topping can be prepared ahead. Just assemble and bake before serving.*

**8 to 10 servings**

3   TABLESPOONS UNSALTED BUTTER

6   TABLESPOONS OLIVE OIL

24  ½-INCH-THICK SLICES
    FRENCH BREAD BAGUETTE

⅓   CUP CHOPPED SHALLOTS
    OR GREEN ONIONS

2   TEASPOONS FINELY
    CHOPPED GARLIC

1½  CUPS CHOPPED PEELED SEEDED
    TOMATOES (ABOUT 2 POUNDS)

¼   CUP CANNED CHICKEN BROTH

¼   TEASPOON DRIED
    CRUSHED RED PEPPER
    SALT

6   COOKED BACON STRIPS,
    CRUMBLED

3   TABLESPOONS MATCHSTICK-SIZE
    STRIPS BASIL

Position rack in center of oven and preheat to 300°F. Melt butter with 3 tablespoons oil in heavy small saucepan over low heat, stirring occasionally. Arrange bread slices on heavy large baking sheet. Brush both sides of bread with butter mixture. Bake until crisp and golden brown, turning once, about 10 minutes. *(Can be prepared 1 day ahead. Cool croutons, then store in plastic bag at room temperature.)*

Heat remaining 3 tablespoons oil in heavy large skillet over medium-high heat. Add shallots and sauté 2 minutes. Add garlic and sauté 1 minute. Mix in tomatoes, broth and dried red pepper. Season with salt. Cook until almost all liquid evaporates, stirring frequently, about 10 minutes. *(Can be prepared 1 day ahead. Transfer mixture to bowl. Cover and refrigerate.)*

Preheat oven to 350°F. Spread tomato mixture over croutons. Top with bacon. Bake until heated through, about 8 minutes. Transfer croutons to platter. Sprinkle with basil.

OPPOSITE: MARMALADE-GLAZED CHICKEN WINGS (TOP); TOMATO CROUTONS WITH BACON AND BASIL AND TOASTED MINI BAGELS WITH SMOKED SALMON AND CAVIAR (BOTTOM).

## Toasted Mini Bagels with Smoked Salmon and Caviar

*These miniature open-face sandwiches are simple to prepare. They look pretty on a bed of dark green spinach leaves.*

**8 to 10 servings**

12 PLAIN MINI BAGELS
¼ CUP (½ STICK) UNSALTED BUTTER, MELTED

FRESH SPINACH LEAVES
SOUR CREAM
4 OUNCES THINLY SLICED SMOKED SALMON
CAVIAR

Preheat oven to 300°F. Halve bagels horizontally using serrated knife. Arrange cut side up on large baking sheet. Brush bagels generously with butter. Bake until light golden brown, about 8 minutes. Cool slightly. *(Can be prepared 3 hours ahead. Cool completely. Wrap tightly; store at room temperature.)*

Arrange spinach decoratively on large platter. Spread each bagel half with sour cream. Cover with salmon. Top with small dollop of sour cream and some caviar. Sprinkle with pepper. Transfer bagels to platter and serve.

## Pickled Shrimp

*In this recipe, the shrimp are lightly pickled in a tangy marinade. Be sure to remove them from the marinade after two hours so that they keep their tender texture.*

**10 servings**

2 CUPS APPLE CIDER VINEGAR
1 ½-INCH PIECE FRESH GINGER, PEELED, THINLY SLICED
2 TABLESPOONS PICKLING SPICE
2 TEASPOONS SALT
½ TEASPOON DRIED CRUSHED RED PEPPER
¼ TEASPOON GROUND MACE
2 POUNDS UNCOOKED EXTRA-LARGE SHRIMP, PEELED, DEVEINED

1 CUP OLIVE OIL
2 LEMONS, CUT INTO ⅛-INCH-THICK SLICES
¾ CUP PLUS 2 TABLESPOONS THINLY SLICED GREEN ONIONS
4 BAY LEAVES
3 GARLIC CLOVES, THINLY SLICED

Combine first 6 ingredients in large skillet over medium-high heat. Bring liquid to simmer. Add shrimp. Remove skillet from heat. Cover pan; let stand until shrimp are opaque in center, about 3 minutes.

Transfer shrimp and vinegar mixture to bowl. Stir in oil, lemon slices, ¾ cup green onions, bay leaves and garlic. Cool. Cover and refrigerate 2 hours.

Using slotted spoon, transfer shrimp to serving bowl. Reserve marinade. *(Can be prepared 1 day ahead. Cover shrimp and marinade separately. Keep refrigerated.)* Arrange lemon slices around edge of bowl. Spoon some of marinade over shrimp. Sprinkle with 2 tablespoons green onions.

## Herbed Phyllo Purses with Camembert and Walnuts

*These delicate cheese- and nut-filled pastries can be prepared the day before. Simply bake until crisp prior to serving.*

**makes about 60**

8 OUNCES CAMEMBERT CHEESE, CUT INTO CUBES WITH RIND, ROOM TEMPERATURE
1 TEASPOON DRIED ROSEMARY
¼ TEASPOON CAYENNE PEPPER
1 EGG, BEATEN TO BLEND
3 TABLESPOONS COARSELY CHOPPED WALNUTS

15 PHYLLO PASTRY SHEETS
1 CUP (2 STICKS) (ABOUT) UNSALTED BUTTER, MELTED

Using electric mixer, beat cheese in small bowl until smooth. Beat in rosemary, cayenne and egg. Mix in nuts.

Butter large baking sheets. Place 1 phyllo sheet on work surface (keep remainder covered with slightly damp towel). Brush phyllo lightly with melted butter. Top with second phyllo sheet. Brush lightly with butter. Top with third phyllo sheet. Brush lightly with butter. Cut stacked, buttered phyllo lengthwise into 3½-inch-wide strips. Then cut crosswise into 3½-inch-wide squares. Place 1 teaspoon cheese filling in center of each square. Gather corners together over center and crimp firmly to form purses. Transfer to prepared sheets, spacing 1 inch apart. Brush tops lightly with butter. Repeat buttering, cutting, filling and crimping with remaining pastry, butter and filling. Refrigerate at least 1 hour. *(Can be prepared 1 day ahead.)*

Preheat oven to 350°F. Bake pastries until crisp and golden brown, about 22 minutes. Cool 5 minutes. Transfer to platter and serve.

## Avocado Pâté with Parsley and Pistachios

*Here's a new guise for the ever-popular guacamole. Cream cheese makes for a richer texture, and it's molded for presentation as a pâté. Make it the day before.*

**8 to 10 servings**

- 4 RIPE AVOCADOS, PITTED, PEELED
- 2 8-OUNCE PACKAGES CREAM CHEESE, ROOM TEMPERATURE
- 2 TABLESPOONS MINCED SHALLOTS OR GREEN ONIONS
- 1 TABLESPOON FRESH LEMON JUICE
- 2 TEASPOONS MINCED GARLIC
- 1 TEASPOON CHILI POWDER
- ½ TEASPOON SALT

- ¼ CUP CHOPPED FRESH PARSLEY
- 2 TABLESPOONS CHOPPED UNSALTED PISTACHIOS
- 4 BUTTER LETTUCE OR BOSTON LETTUCE LEAVES
- ½ CUP PITTED BLACK OLIVES
- 10 RIPE CHERRY TOMATOES TORTILLA CHIPS

Line 6-cup rectangular glass loaf pan or ceramic dish with 3 layers of waxed paper, extending over long sides only. Brush top sheet of paper generously with oil. Puree avocados and cream cheese in processor. Add shallots, lemon juice, garlic, chili powder and salt and blend 30 seconds. Transfer mixture to prepared pan; smooth top. Press plastic wrap onto surface and chill at least 6 hours or overnight.

Remove plastic from pâté. Unmold onto rectangular platter. Remove waxed paper. Mix parsley and pistachios in small bowl. Sprinkle over pâté. Arrange lettuce decoratively at corners of platter. Garnish with olives and tomatoes. Surround with tortilla chips.

ABOVE: HERBED PHYLLO PURSES WITH CAMEMBERT AND WALNUTS.
BELOW: AVOCADO PÂTÉ WITH PARSLEY AND PISTACHIOS.

# NEW YEAR'S EVE DINNER *for* TWO

ROASTED ONION *and* CARROT SOUP

GOAT CHEESE RAVIOLI
*with* WINTER PESTO SAUCE

BROCCOLI

CHAMPAGNE

DEEP-CHOCOLATE GATEAU

## Roasted Onion and Carrot Soup

**2 servings**

1   TABLESPOON OLIVE OIL
12  OUNCES CARROTS, PEELED, CUT INTO ½-INCH-THICK ROUNDS
1   LARGE ONION, CHOPPED

2   GARLIC CLOVES
¼   TEASPOON DRIED THYME
3   CUPS (OR MORE) CANNED LOW-SALT CHICKEN BROTH
    MINCED FRESH CHIVES

Preheat oven to 375°F. Heat oil in heavy large ovenproof skillet over medium-high heat. Add carrots and onion and sauté until onion is tender, about 10 minutes. Transfer skillet to oven and bake until vegetables begin to brown, stirring occasionally, 45 minutes.

Remove skillet from oven; add garlic, thyme and 3 cups broth. Cover and simmer until carrots are very tender, about 30 minutes. Transfer to blender; puree until smooth, adding more broth if too thick. *(Can be made 2 days ahead. Cover; chill.)* Bring to simmer. Ladle into bowls. Garnish with chives.

## Goat Cheese Ravioli with Winter Pesto Sauce

**2 servings**

RAVIOLI

4   GARLIC CLOVES, UNPEELED
1   TEASPOON OLIVE OIL
6   TABLESPOONS SOFT MILD GOAT CHEESE (SUCH AS MONTRACHET)

12  GYOZA (POTSTICKER) WRAPPERS
1   EGG WHITE, BEATEN TO BLEND

PESTO SAUCE

1   TABLESPOON FRESH OREGANO LEAVES
1   TABLESPOON FRESH THYME LEAVES
1   GREEN ONION
1   TEASPOON FRESH ROSEMARY LEAVES
1   GARLIC CLOVE

1   TEASPOON OLIVE OIL
½   CUP CANNED LOW-SALT CHICKEN BROTH
¼   CUP PLUS 1 TABLESPOON WHIPPING CREAM

1   TABLESPOON MINCED FRESH PARSLEY
    GRATED PARMESAN CHEESE

**FOR RAVIOLI:** Preheat oven to 325°F. Place garlic in heavy small skillet. Drizzle with oil and toss to coat. Roast in oven until garlic is very tender, about 25 minutes. Cool. Peel garlic. Combine with goat cheese in small bowl; mash with fork. Season cheese mixture with salt and pepper.

Place gyoza wrappers on work surface. Spoon cheese mixture into center of wrappers. Brush edges of wrappers with egg white. Fold over to form semicircle. Press edges to seal. *(Can be made 1 day ahead. Arrange in single layer on floured baking sheet. Cover tightly and refrigerate.)*

**FOR PESTO SAUCE:** Finely chop first 5 ingredients together. Heat 1 teaspoon oil in heavy medium skillet over medium heat. Add herb mixture; sauté 1 minute. Add broth; increase heat to high and boil until liquid is reduced to 2 tablespoons, about 3 minutes. Add cream. *(Can be made 1 day ahead. Chill.)*

Cook ravioli in large pot of boiling salted water until just tender, about 5 minutes. Drain and divide between 2 bowls. Add parsley to pesto sauce and boil to thicken slightly, about 1 minute. Spoon over ravioli. Sprinkle with cheese.

## Deep-Chocolate Gateau

**2 servings**

CAKE

2½  OUNCES BITTERSWEET CHOCOLATE, CHOPPED
¼   CUP (½ STICK) UNSALTED BUTTER

2   TABLESPOONS SUGAR
2   TABLESPOONS HONEY
1   EXTRA-LARGE EGG
2   TABLESPOONS FINELY CHOPPED TOASTED ALMONDS
¼   TEASPOON VANILLA EXTRACT
⅛   TEASPOON ALMOND EXTRACT
    PINCH OF SALT

GLAZE

¼   CUP WHIPPING CREAM
2   OUNCES BITTERSWEET CHOCOLATE, CHOPPED
1   TABLESPOON HONEY
1   DROP ALMOND EXTRACT

3   TABLESPOONS FINELY CHOPPED TOASTED ALMONDS

**FOR CAKE:** Preheat oven to 325°F. Butter 9 x 5-inch metal loaf pan. Line bottom of pan with parchment paper. Butter parchment. Combine chocolate and butter in heavy small saucepan. Stir over low heat until melted. Cool slightly. Whisk sugar, honey and egg to blend in medium bowl. Stir in chocolate mixture, almonds, vanilla, almond extract and salt. Pour into prepared pan. Bake until tester inserted into center comes out clean, about 30 minutes. *(Cake will be only about ½ inch high.)* Cool 10 minutes in pan. Turn out onto rack; carefully peel off parchment. Cool completely.

**FOR GLAZE:** Bring cream to boil in heavy small saucepan. Remove from heat; add chocolate and stir until melted. Mix in honey and almond extract. Let glaze cool until spreadable, approximately 1¼ hours.

Cut cake crosswise in half. Place 1 half on plate. Spread with 3 tablespoons glaze. Top with second half of cake. Spread top and sides of cake evenly with remaining glaze. Press some almonds onto 2 long sides of cake. Draw tip of knife across top of cake from 1 corner to opposite corner, forming 2 triangles. Sprinkle almonds over top of cake, covering 1 triangle only. Transfer to clean plate. Chill until set. *(Can be made 1 day ahead. Keep chilled.)*

OPPOSITE: ROASTED ONION AND CARROT SOUP AND GOAT CHEESE RAVIOLI WITH WINTER PESTO SAUCE.

# INDEX

# INDEX

# INDEX

# CREDITS & ACKNOWLEDGMENTS

The following people contributed the recipes included in this book:

Bruce Aidells
Mary Barber
Melanie Barnard
Mary Bergin
Davina Besford
Lena Cederham Birnbaum
Carole Bloom
Sara Corpening
Lane Crowther
Randi Danforth
Brooke Dojny
Susan Feniger
Jim Fobel
Gerri Gilliland
Dorie Greenspan
Ken Haedrich
Pam and Jim Heavner
Cheryl and Bill Jamison
Karen Kaplan
Jeanne Thiel Kelley
Kristine Kidd
Sarah Belk King
Lenore Klass
Elinor Klivans
Lakecliff Estate Bed and Breakfast,
   Hood River, Oregon
Connie Larson
Debbie and George Lewis
Michael McLaughlin
Mary Sue Milliken
Jinx and Jefferson Morgan
Selma Brown Morrow
Betty Rosbottom
Patricia Cohen Samuels
Ilana Sharlin
Jordan and Dean Stringfellow
Sarah Tenaglia

The following people contributed the photographs included in this book:

Jack Andersen
Myron Beck
David Bishop
Viktor Budnik
Irene Chang
Katrina De Leon
Julie Dennis
Mark Ferri
Beth Galton
Henry Hamamoto
Charles Imstepf
John Kelly
Michael Lamotte
Brian Leatart
Gabriela Ortuzar
Daniel Ray
Tom Ryan
Jeremy Samuelson
Jeff Sarpa
Mark Thomas

Original photography which appears on pages 8, 12, 40, 43, 58, 61, 86, 92, 100, 146, 152 and the front jacket were done by Mark Thomas. Prop styling for these photographs: Nancy Micklin. Food styling: Dora Johnson. Food styling for front jacket photo: Delores Custer.

Accessories for original photography:

Page 12: Handblown Pilsner Glasses by Simon Pearce, 120 Wooster Street, New York, NY 10012; (212) 334-2393.

Page 40: White Crackle Serving Bowl by Dan Levy, 155 West 29th Street, New York, NY 10001; (212) 268-0878.

Page 146: Crystal Champagne Flutes and Caviar Server available through Baccarat, Inc., 625 Madison Avenue, New York, NY 10022; (212) 826-4100.

Page 152: Ceramic Plates with Gold Rim by Dan Levy (see above). Glass Candleholders and Handblown Glass by Simon Pearce (see above).

**FOR BON APPÉTIT MAGAZINE**

WILLIAM J. GARRY, *Editor-in-Chief*
LAURIE GLENN BUCKLE, *Editor, Bon Appétit Books*
MARCY MACDONALD, *Editorial Business Manager*
CARRI MARKS, *Editorial Production Director*
SYBIL SHIMAZU NEUBAUER, *Editorial Coordinator*
JORDANA RUHLAND, *Assistant Editor*
MARCIA LEWIS, *Editorial Support*
MICHAEL MCLAUGHLIN, *Text*
GAYLEN DUCKER GRODY, *Research*

**FOR CONDÉ NAST BOOKS**

JILL COHEN, *President*
ELLEN MARIA BRUZELIUS, *Division Vice President*
LUCILLE FRIEDMAN, *Fulfillment Manager*
TOM DOWNING, *Direct Marketing Manager*
JILL NEAL, *Direct Marketing Manager*
JENNIFER METZ, *Direct Marketing Associate*
PAUL DINARDO, *Direct Marketing Assistant*

PRODUCED IN ASSOCIATION WITH
PATRICK FILLEY ASSOCIATES, INC.

DESIGNED BY
SALSGIVER COVENEY ASSOCIATES INC.

FRONT JACKET: CRANBERRY-PECAN POUND CAKE (PAGE 13), ORANGE MADELEINES (PAGE 42), PUFF PASTRY PINWHEEL COOKIES WITH JAM (PAGE 143), GOLDEN DELICIOUS APPLE TART (PAGE 95).

Condé Nast Web Address:
http://www.epicurious.com/

Random House Web Address:
http://www.randomhouse.com/